This Little Tiger book belongs to:

Olivia   Sophia

Mommy

Daddy

*For Isobel and Tom ~ D. B.*
*For all the little bears in my world ~ C. P.*

LITTLE TIGER PRESS

1 The Coda Centre, 189 Munster Road, London SW6 6AW
www.littletigerpress.com

First published in Great Britain 2007
by Little Tiger Press, London
This edition published 2012

Printed in China

2 4 6 8 10 9 7 5 3 1

# Bedtime
## for Little Bears!

David Bedford          Caroline Pedler

LITTLE TIGER PRESS

Little Bear and his mother
had spent a long, sunny day
exploring in the snow.

"It's getting late," said Mother Bear. "It will soon be bedtime. Let's go home, Little Bear."

Little Bear flumped down in the snow and wiggled his tail. "I'm not sleepy," he said, "and I don't want to go to bed yet."

Mother Bear smiled. "Shall we take one last walk," she said, "and see who else is going to bed?"

Little Bear looked around. "Who else *is* going to bed?" he wondered.

Mother Bear stretched up tall to find out.

"Look there," she said.

"It's Little Owl!" said Little Bear.

"Little Owl likes to stretch her wings before bedtime, and feel the whisper of the soft night breeze in her feathers," said Mother Bear.

Little Bear scrambled onto his mother's shoulders.

"I like flying, too!" he said.

As Mother Bear climbed to the top of a hill, Little Bear felt the wind whispering and tickling through his fur.

Then he saw someone else . . .

"Who's that?" said Little Bear, giggling.
"And what's he doing?"

"Baby Hare is having a bath in the snow," said Mother Bear, "so that he's clean and drowsy, and ready for sleep."

"I like snow baths, too," said Little Bear. He dived into the snow and scattered it around, plopping a big, soft snowball on Mother Bear's nose.

Little Bear and his
mother laughed as they
flopped down together in
a heap.

"Are you sleepy now, Little Bear?" his mother asked as they lay together in the snow, watching the first bright stars twinkling in the sky.

Little Bear blinked his tired eyes as he tried not to yawn. "I want to see who else is going to bed," he said.

"We'll have to be quiet now," said Mother Bear. "Some little ones will already be asleep."

"Look over there," whispered Mother Bear. "Little Fox likes being cuddled and snuggled to sleep by his mother."

Little Bear pressed close against Mother Bear's warm fur. "I like to cuddle, too," he said.

"We'll be home soon," said his mother softly.

But Little Bear had just seen somebody else . . .

"I can see whales!" he said, turning to look out
across the starlit sea.

"Little Whale likes his mother to sing him softly
to sleep," said Mother Bear.

Little Bear sat with his mother and watched the
whales swimming by until they were gone, leaving
only the soothing hum of their far-away song.
Then he yawned. "Are we nearly home yet?" he
said drowsily.

Little Bear climbed onto his mother's back, and as he was carried home he watched the colors that flickered and brushed across the sky, while his mother sang him a lullaby.

"I like songs, too," he told his mother.

"And now," said Mother Bear very softly, "it's time for little bears to go to sleep."

Little Bear nestled into his mother's soft fur, and when she gave him a gentle kiss goodnight . . .

...Little Bear was
already fast asleep.

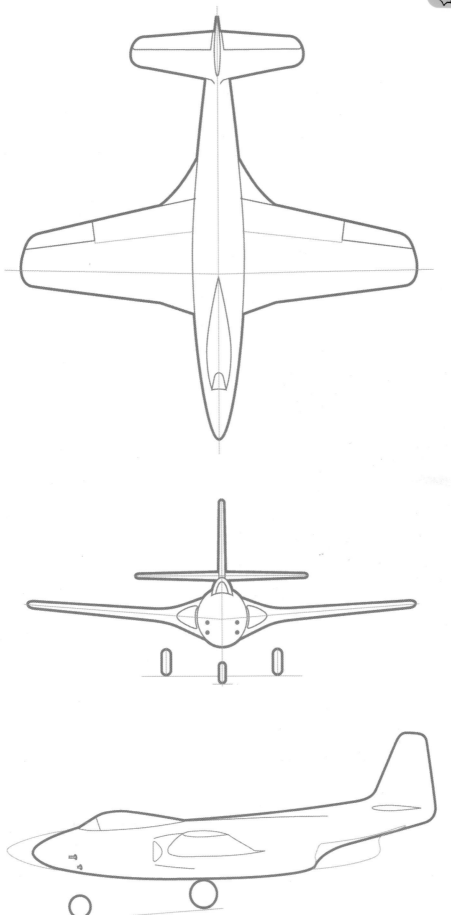

# Grumman F9F Panther/Cougar

## First Grumman Cat of the Jet Age

**Brad Elward**

specialtypress
PUBLISHERS AND WHOLESALERS

**SPECIALTY**press
PUBLISHERS AND WHOLESALERS

Specialty Press
39966 Grand Avenue
North Branch, MN 55056
Phone: 651-277-1400 or 800-895-4585
Fax: 651-277-1203
www.specialtypress.com

Edit by Mike Machat
Layout by Monica Seiberlich

ISBN 978-1-58007-145-1
Item No. SP145

Library of Congress Cataloging-in-Publication Data

Elward, Brad A., 1964-
  Grumman F9F Panther/Cougar: first Grumman cat of the jet age / By Brad Elward.
     p. cm.
  Includes bibliographical references and index.
  ISBN 978-1-58007-145-1
  1.  Panther (Jet fighter plane) 2.  Cougar (Jet fighter plane) 3.  United States. Navy–Aviation–History–20th century.  I. Title.
   UG1242.F5E43725 2010
   623.74'640973–dc22
                                        2010003593

Printed in China
10 9 8 7 6 5 4 3 2 1

**Front Cover:**
*"Hook down! Gear down!" A Grumman F9F-2B Panther is shown landing aboard the USS Antietam (CV-36) during operations off the coast of North Korea in 1951 as part of Task Force 77. Aircraft is wearing the classic early-1950s overall Gloss Sea Blue color scheme as it crosses the carrier's fantail. (Robert Tallman)*

**Title Page:**
*"The thoroughbred." Final production version of the Cougar was the two-seat F9F-8T, used for advanced student flying, carrier qualification, fighter lead-in training, and even as a mock interceptor with AIM-9 Sidewinder missiles as shown here. Refueling probe has been retouched from this photo. (Mike Machat Collection)*

**Inside Front Flap:**
*Grumman's design team at Bethpage, Long Island, celebrates the completion of the modified Design 79D which resembled the production F9F Panther. Added wingtip auxiliary fuel tanks became the aircraft's trademark. (Northrop Grumman History Center)*

**Back Cover, top:**
*Combat-ready swept-wing F9F-8 Cougar rides the deck-edge elevator from the carrier's hangar deck up to the flight deck. This aircraft belongs to Navy Fighter Squadron VF-121 and wears very distinctive red accent markings on nose, tail, and wingtips. (Tommy Thomason)*

**Back Cover, bottom:**
*Dedicated deck hands push an F9F-2B Panther into position on the aircraft carrier USS Princeton (CV-37) before its wings are lowered for launch. It is interesting to note that Grumman's last jet fighter, the 68,000-pound F-14D Tomcat, could only be moved into position with a high-powered tow tractor. (Northrop Grumman Corporation)*

Distributed in the UK and Europe by
Crécy Publishing Ltd
1a Ringway Trading Estate
Shadowmoss Road
Manchester M22 5LH England
Tel: 44 161 499 0024
Fax : 44 161 499 0298
www.crecy.co.uk
enquiries@crecy.co.uk

# TABLE OF CONTENTS

# DEDICATION

This book is dedicated to those at the Grumman Aircraft Company who designed and manufactured the F9F and to all of those members of the United States military who flew and maintained this excellent aircraft.

# PREFACE

Working on *Grumman F9F Panther/Cougar* has been a great experience and one that could not have been possible without the assistance of many individuals. Special thanks are deserving to the Northrop Grumman History Center in Bethpage, New York, and in particular Mr. Larry Feliu and his staff, for hosting my visit this past summer and opening the Grumman Archives, and to Dr. Hill Goodspeed of the Naval Aviation Museum in Pensacola, Florida, who graciously permitted my use of the Museum's wonderful F9F photograph collection.

Thanks also goes to Tommy Thomason, who provided background information and photographs; to Robert F. Dorr, Steve Ginter, Gary Verver, Robert Tallman, Joel Aemselaar, Nick Veronico, Bert Kinzey, and the Tailhook Association, all of whom provided photographs; to aviation photographer Jose Ramos, who ventured to Titusville, Florida, on my behalf and obtained the nice interior images of the Warbirds Air Museum's F9F-5 Panther; to LCDR Rick Burgess (USN ret), for reviewing portions of the manuscript; and to researchers Kevin Morrow and Warren Hower, for their assistance in obtaining information from the National Archives; and to my editor Mike Machat.

I am also grateful to Mr. Walter Spangenberg, a former Panther and Cougar pilot who flew the F9F in Korea; Mr. Royce Williams, who downed at least three MiG-15s during his service in the Korean War; and Mr. Larry Plog, who shot down the first North Korean aircraft of the war for the Navy, each of whom offered his insights—these men are real heroes.

May the Panther and Cougar always be remembered for their tremendous contributions to jet fighter development.

# INTRODUCTION

The story of the Grumman F9F jet fighter is a story of triumph and of perseverance on the part of one of the most successful aircraft manufacturing companies in the world. When Grumman Aircraft turned its attention to jet fighters in 1946, the race to build a viable carrier-borne fighter jet aircraft was already well underway. Indeed, for a time, it looked like many of its industry competitors—McDonnell, North American, and Douglas—would be the forerunners of the fledgling industry. Yet, Grumman's F9F-2 Panther emerged on the scene in 1947 and soon became the most numerous jet fighter on the deck of U.S. Navy aircraft carriers. Moreover, it would prove to be the premier Navy fighter of the Korean War, becoming the first Navy jet to claim an enemy aircraft, the first Navy jet to score a kill against the venerable Soviet MiG-15, and the first Navy jet to be adapted for air-to-ground operations. During the war, the Panther achieved no less than seven official kills and two unofficial kills, and, through the F9F-2B and F9F-5, took the lead in the Navy's close air support role.

The swept-wing Cougar variant was introduced as a result of the Panther's encounters with the MiG-15. With the F9F-6, the Cougar became the fleet's primary air defense fighter and also attack aircraft for the early part of the 1950s. Later, the much improved F9F-8 and F9F-8B became the premier variant of the F9F series, capable of Mach 1+ speeds in a dive and carrying the new AIM-9 Sidewinder heat-seeking air-to-air missile. It could also carry low-yield nuclear weapons. In fact, the Cougar was the first Navy fighter to operationally deploy with the AIM-9, when it made its first deployment aboard a carrier on a Mediterranean cruise in 1956.

In all, 3,370 F9Fs were built in 13 variants, including four photoreconnaissance versions, the F9F-2P, F9F-5P, F9F-6P, and F9F-8P, and the two-seat F9F-8T, in a production run that lasted 13 years, from 1947 through 1960. All variants were built at Grumman's Bethpage, Long Island, New York, facilities. Panther variants saw action in Korea at some point between 1950 and 1953 and the F9F-8T saw limited action in Vietnam flying Tactical Air Control (TAC) (Airborne) missions with Marine Corps squadron H&MS-13. The Cougar was also responsible for training most of the naval aviators who flew in Vietnam. Throughout its career, the F9F was known as a rugged, reliable, and an easy-to-fly aircraft that brought many pilots home with damage that in many cases would have doomed other aircraft.

The Panther and Cougar served in both active and reserve U.S. Navy and Marine Corps squadrons and several test squadrons, plus formed the core of the Naval Air Training Command as a single-seat and dual-seat trainer. The last operational F9F, an F9F-8T with VT-4, was retired in February 1974, marking the end of an outstanding 25-year service career. The F9F represents a significant step in naval aviation history and will long be regarded as one of the most capable jet fighters of its day.

# CHAPTER ONE

# THE DEVELOPMENT OF POSTWAR JET AIRCRAFT

*Naval aviation in the early years of the Jet Age is represented in this Naval Air Test Center formation. Illustrating various configurations from several different manufacturers, we see (from bottom) the twin-tail Vought F7U Cutlass fighter, McDonnell F2H-1 Banshee, Grumman F9F-2 Panther, and Vought F6U Pirate. Only the Banshee and Panther ever saw combat action during the Korean War.* (U.S. Navy via Tailhook Association)

No discussion of the Grumman F9F Panther/Cougar would be complete unless it began with an overview of the environment from which the aircraft emerged. At the time the F9F was conceived, the United States Army Air Force (USAAF) and the U.S. Navy were in a period of transition from high-performance propeller-driven aircraft to the era of jet propulsion. On the heels of five years of war, U.S. fighters of both services were at their peak level of performance, with aircraft such as the Republic P-47D Thunderbolt and North American P-51D Mustang serving in USAAF squadrons and the Grumman F6F Hellcat, F8F Bearcat, and Vought F4U Corsair flying with the Navy carrier squadrons.

The story of the development of jet aircraft really amounts to a tale of the development of jet propulsion. As is explained more fully in the following pages, the development of the first usable turbojet engines occurred on nearly parallel tracks during the mid-1930s and early 1940s in Germany and the United Kingdom (UK).[i] The United States, which had concentrated its aeronautical industry on gearing up production for the impending war and on producing the most capable versions of current technologies, lagged considerably behind Germany and the UK and did not seriously pursue jet engine development until the middle of World War II. Moreover, once the decision was made to pursue the turbojet, it was the USAAF that led the way in 1941, with the Navy following suit in 1943.

The F9F represents one of the most successful second-generation carrier-based jet aircraft. The F9F developed in the midst of rapidly advancing technology, which moved so fast that aircraft were often obsolete by the time they were ready for production or fleet deployment. In the same sense, the role of the fighter was likewise evolving from that of fleet defense and escort to highly specialized missions such as night fighter and interceptor and the emerging fighter-bomber. With the advent of long-range bombers and the potential threats they posed to carrier task forces, long-range interception took on a new importance.

Early interest in the turbine focused largely on steam-turbine design, with little focus on its application to other fields. In the early part of the 1900s, the British successfully harnessed steam turbine technology for use in ships and quickly incorporated it into military and then commercial designs. Work also proceeded on using turbines for superchargers applied to aircraft piston-engines to improve their performance at higher altitudes. It was not until the 1920s that research began focusing on the use of gas turbine engines as a means of jet propulsion rather than an enhancement to reciprocating engine designs.

## Britain's Frank Whittle and the Jet Engine

Frank Whittle has often been referred to as the father of jet propulsion.[ii] Whittle was born in 1907 and became a Royal Air Force (RAF) officer in the late 1920s. He had a tremendous interest in engineering and in 1929, as part of his officer training graduation thesis, postulated the concept of jet propulsion as a means to accomplish high-speed, high-altitude flight. Whittle continued to pursue his ideas and eventually developed the concept for the basic jet turbine engine. Despite the potential of the design, the British Air Ministry passed on the idea and Whittle set about developing the engine on his own.

By 1935, Whittle had begun his first prototype engine called the Whittle Unit (W.U.). The engine was successfully bench-tested in April 1937 and again in June 1939, an event which finally caught the attention of the British government. As a result, the Air Ministry offered Whittle funding for the development of a flyable version of the engine and also authorized development of an experimental aircraft to flight test the engine. Whittle thus began work on the Whittle Supercharger Type W.1 (called simply the W.1) and in 1940, Gloster, which had been given charge of the airframe contract, set about design of the E.28/39. A second engine contract was also placed for a larger turbojet design, which would develop into the W.2.

The E.28/39 underwent taxi tests on 7 April 1941 powered by the W.1X, an experimental design Whittle had hastily made while his manufacture of the W.1 experienced delays.[iii] The taxi tests consisted of several short hops of several hundred yards and achieved flight at about six feet off the ground. By May, the W.1 was completed and the E.28/39 made its maiden flight on the 15th, marking Britain's first flight of a jet-powered aircraft. The aircraft flew for 17 minutes and reached a maximum speed of 340 mph (547 km/h). Only a few days later, the E.28/39 topped 370 mph (595 km/h) at 25,000 feet, a speed already exceeding that of the much-heralded Spitfire. Whittle's W.1 produced 850 lbf (pounds of

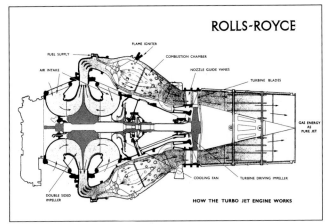

ROLLS-ROYCE

This cutaway shows the basic design and airflow of a centrifugal compressor turbojet engine. The air enters the air intakes and is altered vertically where it contacts the double-sided impeller and then mixes with fuel to create ignition. (Rolls Royce)

Rolls-Royce was one of Britain's leading jet engine designers and was responsible for the legendary Merlin engine, which powered the Hawker Hurricane, Supermarine Spitfire, and de Havilland Mosquito. The Derwent centrifugal compressor turbojet (shown here) was an improved version of the Welland engine, a derivative of Frank Whittle's original design. The 2,000-pound (8.9 kN) thrust Derwent powered the Gloster Meteor. (Rolls-Royce)

The British were among the first to develop a working, operational jet fighter. Work on the Gloster Meteor began in November 1940 in conjunction with efforts to produce an operational jet engine from Frank Whittle's initial prototypes. The Meteor was delivered to the Royal Air Force (RAF) in June 1944 and was the only jet fighter to serve with the Allies during the war. It served with No. 616 Squadron and was used to counter German V-1 flying bombs. (National Archives via Warren Hower)

thrust) (3.8 kN). His next design, the W.2 (although by then production had been taken over by Rolls-Royce as the W.2B/23 Welland), would power the twin-engine Gloster Meteor, Britain's first operational jet fighter. The Meteor, first flown in 1943, entered service in RAF squadrons in July 1944.

### Germany's Jet Engine Programs

Unbeknownst to Whittle, the German aircraft industry during the 1930s was proceeding with the development of its own jet engine programs and at a very rapid pace. Indeed, as of the late 1930s the German industry was ahead of even the British. The German path to the jet engine started with the work of a young engineer/physicist, Hans von Ohain, who in 1933 wrote his thesis at University of Göttingen, one of Germany's leading aeronautical centers, describing the basics of "an engine that did not require a propeller."[iv] Ohain's work continued after graduation and in 1935, working with an automotive engineer, Max Hahn, he built a prototype of the design in Hahn's automotive garage. Ohain patented his version of the jet engine in 1936 and later that year caught the attention of one of

The Messerschmitt Me-262 was the most successful of the World War II jet designs. It served operationally from June 1944 through the end of the war, although never in sufficient numbers to significantly alter the course of the war. The Me-262 was well ahead of its time and had many features, such as its swept-wing design, which would later be incorporated into all modern jet fighters. The Me-262 was reverse engineered by both American and Soviet engineers and led to the MiG-15 Fagot and F-86 Sabre fighters. (National Archives via Warren Hower)

Germany's leading aircraft designers, Ernst Heinkel, who immediately hired both Ohain and Hahn. Once at Heinkel, Ohain modified and refined his work, the result being the Heinkel-Strahltriebwerk 1 (HeS 1). Completed in 1937, the centrifugal-flow engine was constructed of sheetmetal. Although the first engine was tested using hydrogen, the HeS 1 was converted into a gas turbine in September, due to damage caused by the high temperatures associated with burning hydrogen. A flight-quality design followed the HeS 3, which was constructed of machined parts, and subsequently the improved HeS 3b. The HeS 3, which constituted the first usable jet engine and was rated at 1,100 lbf, ran for the first time in mid-1939, just one month prior to Whittle's design. It was then installed in the He 178 test airframe, which flew on 27 August 1939, marking the first ever flight of a jet-powered aircraft.

At about the same time, Junkers Motoren (Jumo) was beginning work on an axial flow turboprop design, the Jumo 004A, as was BMW with its Model 003. Both companies had received their funding in 1938-39 from Helmut Schelp, the German Air Minister, with instructions to focus their efforts on axial-flow designs which offered higher efficiency as well as smaller diameter and lower drag versus the centrifugal design. Ironically, Messerschmitt likewise began work on the preliminary design of what would become the Me-262 Schwalbe ("Swallow"), the world's first combat operational jet

*A collection of aircraft from VC-3 includes (from bottom) the F6F Hellcat, two F4U Corsairs, the F3D Skyknight, and two F2H-1 Banshees. The Hellcat was the Navy's premier carrier fighter during World War II and the Corsair, which flew largely for Marine units during World War II, also flew thousands of combat missions in Korea. The two piston-engined fighters are shown here with two of the early U.S. Navy jet fighters.* (U.S. Navy via Tailhook Association)

# CENTRIFUGAL-FLOW, AXIAL-FLOW, AND SUPERCHARGER DESIGN[V]

Jet engines are simply a slang term for gas turbine engines, all of which rely on compressors to increase the pressure of the incoming air before it enters the burner portion. Given this function, the compressor performance therefore has a great impact of the overall efficiency of the engine. There are two principle types of compressors—centrifugal and axial. Generally speaking, in a centrifugal compressor the air flowing through the compressor is projected perpendicular to the axis of rotation. An axial compressor features air flowing parallel to the axis of rotation.

Early jet engines, such as the Nene, featured centrifugal compressors, which are simple to manufacture and are relatively inexpensive to produce. However, they cannot achieve the high compression ratio without becoming exceptionally large. Axial flow compressors, in contrast, are highly efficient and possess a large mass flow capacity. Axial flow compressors existed in the early 1900s but were not efficient and thus, deemed impractical. However, in the mid-1920s research discovered that the poor performance could be attributed to the use of flat blades within the compressors. These were replaced with airfoils, which produced dramatic improvements. It was not until the late 1930s, however, that significant progress was made by the English Metropolitan Vickers (Metrovick). Similar efforts emerged in Germany by Junkers with its work on the Jumo 004, and by BMW with its BMW 003. Although centrifugal compressors continued into the early 1950s, the axial compressor became the industry standard.

Another form of compressor can be found with the supercharger used in piston-driven engines to allow operation at high altitudes. Standard engines experience decreased performance as the aircraft climbs to higher altitudes because the air density surrounding the engine decreases. As a result of the lower air intake, the engine produces less power. Superchargers compress the air surrounding an engine back to sea level pressures or higher, which, in the lower drag environment of high altitude, allows the aircraft to attain even higher speeds.

fighter. The jet-powered Me-262 made its first flight on 18 July 1942 using the 1,980 lbf (8.8 kN) Jumo 004B.

Thus, by the end of 1941, the Germans and the British were well on their way to successfully fielding usable jet engine designs and aircraft capable of taking those engines into battle. The Germans had four jet engines in development, two by Heinkel, the Jumo 004, and the BMW 003, and two jet fighter designs, the Me-262 and the He-280. Likewise, the British were working on a second variation of Whittle turbojet design as well as the Gloster Meteor.

### The U.S. Aeronautical Industry Starts and Stops

While the U.S. aeronautical industry during the 1930s did not fully appreciate the potential of jet propulsion, it cannot be said that the concept of jet power was a complete unknown. Several companies were conducting experiments with the steam turbine for heavy industrial use, superchargers for piston engines, and in heat-resistant alloys. All of these technologies would eventually come to benefit the American effort to develop jet propulsion once the Army Air Force made the decision to head in that direction.

Part of the perceived lack of U.S. interest in the turbojet designs was the result of the engineering culture prevalent at that time.[vi] First, there was a dramatic difference between how science approached innovation in the United States and in Europe. In Europe, German and British engineers and physicists were heavily entrenched in theoretical science, which encouraged

*Lockheed produced a very effective turbofan engine, the L-1000 (T36), which was originally designed as a turbojet engine in the mid-to-late 1930s. The L-1000 was intended to be used in Lockheed's L-133 Starjet design, which was never built. Although a contract for construction of the L-1000 and L-133 was let in 1941, it was quickly cast aside by the more advanced British designs being delivered to the Americans as part of the information and technology exchange following the Tizard Mission.* (National Archives via Warren Hower)

fundamental research into new aerodynamics. American scientists were extremely empirical and utilitarian and focused not on theory, but on practical solutions to present problems. Thus, American researchers looked for ways to improve existing designs through "incremental refinements to existing technology," enhancing performance and efficiency.

Second, the philosophy of the Army Air Corps procurement system during the 1920s and 1930s supported a more practical approach. Indeed, few if any pure research and development contracts were issued. Aircraft and engine companies were expected to ingest the costs of all research or to recoup it in their ultimate program budgets. Radical designs were not encouraged. This philosophy further crystallized during the prewar and war years, when the American aeronautical industry had been instructed to concentrate their efforts on enhancing and maximizing the production of existing aircraft. Interestingly, the Army Air Force had been presented with a research report in August 1939 setting forth the need to conduct further research into gas turbine or rocket propulsion systems because transonic flight (faster than the sound barrier) was not possible with propeller-driven aircraft technology. That report, entitled "Air Corps Materiel Division Engineering Section Memorandum Report 50-461-351" and submitted by Ezra Kotcher, a senior instructor at the Army Corps Engineering School, was largely ignored.

That being so, General Electric put much of its efforts into designing steam turbines and applying supercharger technology to radial engines for high-altitude bombers.[vii] Northrop Corporation had also begun work on its T37 Turbodyne, which would later become the United States' first turboprop design for bomber aircraft. Perhaps the most significant developments in turbojet engines came from aircraft manufacturer Lockheed, through the designs of engineer Nathan C. Price. Price began work on a turbojet design in late 1938 and was eventually asked by Lockheed's Skunk Works to develop an engine for the experimental high-speed, high-altitude XP-49 (a derivative of the XP-38 Lightning). During 1941, Lockheed ordered a new aircraft, the L-133, powered by Price's new engine, which was designated as the L-1000 (XJ37 internally). The L-1000 design called for a sea-level thrust of 5,100 lbf (22,700 N) and weighed 1,700 pounds (775 kg). Moreover, the proposal promised a top speed of 625 mph at 50,000 feet. Both proposals were submitted by Lockheed to the Army Air Corps' development division at Wright Field, but were met with little interest. Army policy at the time prohibited use of an airframe and engine from the same manufacturer; moreover, the L-133's stainless-steel canard design was regarded as being too radical.

The Army Air Corp revisited the engine proposal in July 1943 and issued a long-term development contract for delivery of an L-1000 in 1945.[viii] However, upon delivery the Army revised its requirements and called for a turboprop design. Lockheed complied and produced the J37/T35, delivering three working engines. However, the Air Force decided not to pursue this engine and turned over the turboprop engines and all test data to the aeronautical industry as a whole.

## "Hap" Arnold Brings the Whittle Engine to the United States

As noted earlier, on 7 April 1941, the British took one step closer to achieving Whittle's dream of jet flight when the Gloster E.28/39 underwent its initial taxi tests. At that test was one man who would have a tremendous impact on the future of jet development in the United States. Gen. Henry "Hap" Arnold, Chief of the Army Air Force, had been visiting England and had been shown the plans for the Gloster G.40 Pioneer jet aircraft as well as Whittle's Model W.2B turbojet engine. Gen. Arnold was reportedly "stunned" by the advancements made by the British since he had first learned of their jet experiments in the fall of 1940 during the so-called "Tizard Mission." In September 1940 during the peak of the Battle of Britain, a UK scientific delegation visited the United States to both share high-level military technology and to take advantage of the significantly greater American production capabilities.[ix]

Officially called the British Technical and Scientific Mission, Sir Henry Tizard served as the leader of the delegation and brought with him information concerning some of Britain's most advanced technology, such as radar (a highly advanced cavity magnetron), details of Frank Whittle's jet engine, and the Frisch-Peierls memorandum, which outlined the feasibility of the atomic bomb, as well as other smaller advances, such as submarine detection devices and self-sealing fuel tanks. Tizard's goal was to trade information on these technologies for certain American technology, such as the American Norden bombsight. The mission was ultimately dubbed a success, with Tizard's efforts leading to the development of advanced radar, LORAN navigation, as well as cementing the foundations of the Anglo-American alliance.

Based on the information exchanged as part of the Tizard Mission as well as information concerning Germany's jet engine advances, Gen. Arnold organized a high-level scientific commission in late February 1941 under the auspices of the National Advisory Committee for Aeronautics (NACA) to study jet propulsion. The Committee, which was lead by the renowned, but aged, scientist Dr. William F. Durand, began its work in April 1941, but was quickly superseded by the news Arnold brought back from England later that month.

Upon his return to the States, Arnold immediately summoned representatives from General Electric to develop a jet engine along the lines of the British Whittle design. Yet given the British lead in the technology, Gen. Arnold and the NACA committee determined it made more sense to simply license British designs. GE's turbocharger division at Lynn, Massachusetts, was chosen for the task because the other U.S. engine manufacturers were heavily committed to prewar prop-engine production. By September, the Army Air Force had approved development of the first U.S. jet fighter, which it asked Bell Aircraft to construct. The aircraft, known as the XP-59, would feature a GE-built version of the Whittle W.2B engine.

### The USAAF Jet Developments

On 30 September 1941, a Letter Contract was issued to Bell Aircraft calling for three experimental jet-powered aircraft, which Bell had designated as the Bell Model

*The Bell Aircraft XP-59A Airacomet marked the United States' entry into the Jet Age. The XP-59A first flew in October 1942 and its performance proved to be lacking. However, the design helped pave the way for other American jet fighters and provided jet experience to pilots and naval aviators who would go on to fly the first- and second-generation jet fighters. Three XP-59As were built, followed by 13 YP-59As, 20 P-59As, and 30 P-59Bs. One YP-59 was given to the RAF in 1944 in exchange for a Meteor.* (National Archives via Warren Hower)

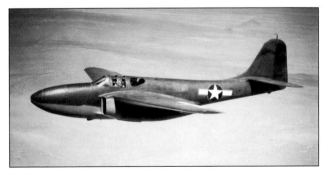

*Bell's XP-59A (Model 27) was given the same designation as the radial-piston engine XP-59 to disguise it from prying foreign eyes. The XP-59A was the first jet-propelled aircraft produced in the United States.* (Tommy Thomason)

*A McDonnell FH-1 Phantom from VMF-122 sits on the tarmac at Marine Corps Air Station (MCAS) Cherry Point, North Carolina, in 1947. The aircraft had a rather short operational history and was quickly replaced by the more capable F2H-1 Banshee.* (U.S. Navy via Tailhook Association)

*This collection of early Navy jets represents the first and second generations of Navy jet fighters. Shown here, from front-to-back in echelon formation, are the North American FJ-1 Fury, Grumman XF9F-2 Panther, McDonnell F2H-1 Banshee, and McDonnell FH-1 Phantom.* (U.S. Navy via Tailhook Association)

XP-67 Bat for the Army Air Corps, the Navy ordered three of the proposed fighter designs on 30 August, designating it as the XFD-1. The XFD-1 mounted four 0.50 Caliber machine guns in its nose, but had no provisions for external ordnance. Powered by two Westinghouse J30-WE-20 turbojets, each with 1,600 lbf (7.1 kN), the Phantom was the first Navy jet to reach speeds over 500 mph. The first Phantom flew on 26 January 1946 and marked history as the first U.S. pure jet carrier landing on 21 July that year aboard USS *Franklin D. Roosevelt* (CVB-42).

While performing better than Navy piston-driven fighters of the day, the Phantom lacked the performance of other jet fighters fielded by the USAF and those of potential adversaries. Only 66 Phantoms were built, with one squadron, VF-17A (later redesignated as VF-171) entering service. Phantoms also were assigned to Marine Corps squadrons VMF-122 and -311. The Phantom would prove a good first step in the procession to high-performance jet fighters, but was quickly surpassed by the entry of second-generation aircraft such as the McDonnell F2H-1 Banshee and the Grumman F9F-2 Panther. After 1949, Phantoms were relegated to training roles and to the Naval Reserve squadrons. Interestingly, no FH-1 squadron ever deployed for a full-length operational cruise.

*On 7 July 1946, the Navy launched its first jet-powered fighter, the McDonnell FH-1 Phantom, from the deck of the USS* Franklin D. Roosevelt *(CVB-42). The aircraft is shown here on the deck of the USS* Coral Sea *(CVB-43) later that same year. The FH-1 began serving in operational Navy squadrons (VF-17A) in August 1947 and with VMF-122 in November. In May 1948, VF-17A became the first Navy squadron to deploy with a jet fighter when it went to sea aboard USS* Saipan *(CVL-48).* (U.S. Navy via Tailhook Association)

As jet engines and jet fighter research continued, the Navy explored a composite design that combined the traditional radial engine and a turbojet engine in a single airframe. The thought was to take advantage of each powerplant's benefits at different stages of flight. The Ryan FR-1 Fireball was one of the composite aircraft designs built in the 1940s. It featured a 1,350-hp Wright Cyclone R-1820-72W radial engine in the nose and the General Electric I-16 (J31) centrifugal turbojet engine mounted in the rear. The FR-1 first flew on 20 September 1944 and was used by two Navy squadrons, VF-66 and VF-41 (VF-1E). They were withdrawn from service in mid-1947 as the first generation of jet fighters reached the fleet. (U.S. Navy via Tailhook Association)

### The Navy Experiments With Composite Aircraft

As jet development progressed, the Navy experimented with a compromise design, the so-called composite aircraft, which combined a jet engine and a propeller engine in a single aircraft. The intention was to use the propeller for initial takeoff and landing, where slower speeds and quicker engine reaction times were critical, and to use the jet engine to rapidly ingress the area of action and for combat. The first composite contract went to a small company named Ryan Aeronautical Corporation of San Diego, California. The Navy had issued a request for proposal in December 1942 to nine manufacturers calling for composite submissions. One of those nine companies, Ryan, convinced the Navy that it could meet the challenge and was awarded a contract in February 1943. Interestingly, Ryan had no experience working for the Navy or in fighter design. However, Ryan was the only manufacturer of the nine that was not fully engaged with existing war production contracts.

The contract called for Ryan to produce three prototype aircraft of the Ryan Model 28, to be designated as the XFR-1, plus a single static airframe.[xiv] The XFR-1s were to have stall, takeoff, and landing speeds based on air operations aboard the smaller escort carriers (CVEs). The XFR-1 was a single-seat, low-wing monoplane configuration offering the first laminar-flow airfoil specifically designed for carrier use. In another first for carrier aviation, it had all flush welded exterior and all-metal control surfaces. A Wright Cyclone R-1820-72W

nine-cylinder, air-cooled radial engine was mounted in the nose, providing 1,350 hp. A General Electric I-16 (J31) centrifugal flow jet engine providing 1,600 lbf was located behind the cockpit in a centerline mount.

During manufacture of the prototypes, the Navy issued a production contract for 100 FR-1s, by then named the Fireball. The first XFR-1 (BuNo 48232) was

Curtiss Aircraft also entered the mix for a composite fighter, producing the XF15C. First flown in February 1945, it was similar to the Ryan Fireball, but lacked the performance. Powered by the 2,700-lbf (12.26 kN) Allis-Chalmers J36, it was in theory to be the fastest fighter in Navy service at that time. The first aircraft built is shown here on its maiden flight on 27 February 1945. This example crashed on 8 May that year. Only three prototypes were built and the Navy eventually canceled the contract. (U.S. Navy via Tailhook Association)

delivered in late May 1944 and took to the skies on 25 June, although the jet engine had yet to be installed. Full flight testing with both the propeller and jet engines took place in July. A contract for 600 FR-1s was issued, but was canceled after V-J Day, leaving only 66 aircraft as having been produced. Although offering many advantages in handling over the propeller aircraft of the day (the FR-1 could out-turn all propeller aircraft and had a roll-rate twice that of the nimble German FW-190), the Ryan aircraft was eventually canceled. One squadron, VF-66, was equipped with the Fireball and deployed in late 1945. Although VF-66 was subsequently decommissioned, its personnel and aircraft were transferred to VF-41 (later VF-1E) and deployed aboard several escort carriers, including USS *Wake Island* (CVE-65), USS *Bairoko* (CVE-115), and USS *Badoeng Strait* (CVE-116).

Curtiss had also tendered a composite aircraft, the XF15C.[xv] The Navy had issued a contract on 7 April 1944 calling for three prototypes using the 2,100-hp Pratt & Whitney R-2800 piston engine and the Allis-Chalmers 2,700-lbf (12.26 kN) J36 turbojet. The J36 was an Americanized version of the de Havilland Halford H-1B. The design first flew on 27 February 1945, although without its jet engine, and reached a top speed of 373 mph. With the jet engine operating, the XF15C registered a top speed of 469 mph and achieved a range of 1,385 miles. Although the initial prototype was destroyed in a crash, the two remaining prototypes were subsequently delivered and service test flights had commenced; however, the program was canceled in October 1946, the decision having been made that the future of carrier aviation was in jet propulsion.

# U.S. NAVY FIGHTER DESIGNATION SYSTEM

The U.S. Navy fighter designation system[xvi] from 1922 until 1962 was a complex and often confusing system that classified naval aircraft based on manufacture, type, and model sequence. Prior to 1922, the service had no unified designation scheme, relying instead on the designation given to the aircraft by the manufacturer.

On 29 March 1922, however, the Navy adopted a uniform classification system, which prevailed until 1962, when all services were placed under a uniform designation system by the Department of Defense. The basic Navy post-1922 system worked as follows:

(Status prefix) (Type)(Manufacturer type sequence) (Manufacturer)—(Configuration sequence number) (Special purpose suffix)

According to the Navy's system, the "type" denoted the aircraft's role or mission, such as "F" for fighter, "TB" for torpedo bomber, or "S" for scout. Each manufacturer was assigned a one-letter (or on occasion, two-letter) code; Grumman Aircraft Engineering Corporation, for example, was assigned the letter "F"; the letter "J" was assigned to North American Aviation Corporation after 1937. General Motors Corporation's Eastern Aircraft Division, which manufactured Wildcats and Avengers under license from Grumman, was assigned the letter "M."

The manufacturer type sequence number represented the procurement sequence of the particular model ordered from a given manufacturer. To use Grumman as an example, the first Navy fighter ordered from Grumman was designated as FF-1, followed by F2F-1 for the second fighter ordered and F3F-1 for the third. Likewise, the first fighter ordered from North American was designated as the FJ-1. In a similar manner, the aircraft configuration sequence number informed of the different modifications within the same aircraft design. As an illustration, the Grumman F4F Wildcat was ordered in several variants or modifications, designated as F4F-2 through the F4F-8.

The final two terms represent the aircraft's status prefix and its special purpose suffix. The status prefix was placed in front of the class designation and indicated whether the aircraft was experimental (designated by an "X") or a service test aircraft (designated by a "Y"). Thus, the prototype F9F Panther was designated as the XF9F-2; a service test aircraft would be denoted as YF9F-2. A special purpose designation was typically given for an aircraft modified for a particular mission, such as photoreconnaissance or night fighter. Again as an example, the photoreconnaissance version of the Panther was referenced as the F9F-2P or the F9F-5P, while a night fighter variant of the Vought Corsair would be designated as F4U-5N.

This designation system prevailed until 16 September 1962, when the Department of Defense, at the insistence of then-Secretary of Defense Robert S. McNamara, introduced a common designation system for all military aircraft, covering not only the Navy, but also the Air Force and Marines. Under this system, a McDonnell F4H Phantom (Navy and Marine Corps)/F-110 Spectre (Air Force) was simply referred to as the F-4 Phantom II regardless of the service branch.

While the Navy pursued a straight-winged FJ-1 for its carrier decks, the Air Force pursued the swept-wing version, called the XF-86, which became the Sabre. The Sabre was later modified for carrier use, becoming the FJ-3 Fury. (Tommy Thomason)

Two McDonnell F2H-1P photoreconnaissance aircraft can be seen here wearing VMJ-1 markings. The photo Banshee was on order when the Navy converted some of the F9F-2 Panther lot to the -2P standard to fill the immediate need for a jet photoreconnaissance aircraft during the Korean War. (U.S. Navy via Tailhook Association)

The North American FJ-1 Fury came in response to the Navy's 1944 Request for Proposal for a jet-powered day fighter. The Fury's contract came at approximately the same time as those for the XFD-2 (F2H) Banshee and XF6U Pirate. The Air Force pursued a swept-wing version of the Fury, which became the F-86 Sabre. The FJ-1 was assigned to VF-5A and made its first deployment aboard USS Boxer (CV-21). (U.S. Navy via Tailhook Association)

The Chance Vought F6U Pirate is trailed by an FH-1 and F2H-1 as seen in 1950. The F6U Pirate was Vought's proposal for a jet-powered day fighter. It made its first flight on 2 October 1946, with Vought test pilot Ted Owens at the controls. The Pirate proved so sub-marginal in performance that operational use was deemed unfeasible and the program was canceled. (U.S. Navy via Tailhook Association)

FJ-1 (BuNo 120347) sits on the tarmac at the Naval Air Test Center during the aircraft's flight testing phase. During one spin test flight the aircraft's canopy came off and knocked the pilot unconscious. When he came to, the aircraft was going through a series of slow rolls. He eventually regained control and landed safely. Although 100 FJ-1s were ordered, only 30 of the straight-wing Furies were ever built. (U.S. Navy via Tailhook Association)

## Navy Test Flights in Army Air Corps Jets

The Navy gained its initial jet experience at the controls of Army Air Corps P-59As, originally designated as the F2L-1 by BuAer. Beginning in 1943, the Navy obtained five Airacomets, two YP-59As (42-108778, 42-108779), and three P-59Bs (44-22651, 44-22656, and 44-22657). These were subsequently given the BuNos 63960, 63961, 64100, 64108, and 64109. The first YP-59 (63960) arrived at Naval Air Test Center (NATC) Patuxent River in November 1943, with the second arriving in December. The first P-59B, aircraft 64100, arrived on 17 October 1945, followed by the second, aircraft 64108, on 15 January 1946, and the third, aircraft 64109, on 12 February 1946.

Capt. Frederick M. Trapnell, Chief of Flight Test at the Navy's Bureau of Aeronautics (BuAer), became the first naval aviator to pilot a jet on 21 April 1943 during a flight of the first XP-59A at Muroc. Cdr. Paul H. Ramsey followed on 29 July that same year. The Navy used the P-59s as training aircraft and began transitioning naval aviators into jet pilots at NATC. By November

*A formation of four McDonnell F2H-1 Banshees flies over the USS Coral Sea (CVB-43).* (U.S. Navy via Tailhook Association)

manufacturers to submit designs.[xvii] Four manufacturers responded—Grumman, McDonnell, North American, and Chance Vought—resulting in the eventual selection of three proposals for development. The first contract was issued in September for production of the Chance Vought XF6U Pirate. McDonnell, which had already been working on the FH-1 Phantom, received the second contract in November for the XFD-2 (F2H) Banshee. Finally, a contract was issued to North American Aircraft in January 1945 for the Model NA-135, designated as the XFJ-1 Fury. Of interest, the Army was also pursuing a variant of the XFJ-1, known as the XP-86, which, with addition of a swept-wing design, became the venerable F-86 Sabre of Korean War fame. Grumman and its Design 71 were bypassed.

1944, the Navy was transitioning three pilots per day. Interestingly, of the first 231 Navy jet pilots, all but 48 were jet qualified in a P-59.

### The 1944 Naval Jet Fighter Request For Proposal

By 1944, the notion of a carrier-borne jet fighter was widely accepted and BuAer issued a new requirement for a carrier jet fighter, asking eight of the leading aircraft

The Fury was a straight-winged aircraft powered by a single Allison J35-A-2 (originally the GE TG-180) and armed with six nose-mounted .50-cal. machine guns. Although delivered to the Navy in January 1946, it came without an engine and did not achieve first flight until September 1946. A production order for 100 FJ-1s was issued in May 1945 and the Fury was delivered to VF-5A

*The Lockheed P-80 Shooting Star was the first operational U.S. jet fighter, serving with the U.S. Army Air Force. The Navy obtained several Lockheed P-80 Shooting Stars for training and redesignated them as TO-2s. This one carries the markings of the Naval Air Test Center (NATC) at Patuxent River, Maryland.* (National Archives via Warren Hower)

# GRUMMAN AIRCRAFT ENGINEERING CORPORATION

Grumman Aircraft Engineering Corporation was incorporated on 6 December 1929 by Leroy Grumman and four friends; Bill Schwendler, Jake Swirbul, Edmund W. Poor, and E. Clinton Towl. Grumman and several of his partners had worked for the Loening Aircraft Engineering Corporation during the 1920s, until the company was merged in 1928 with the Keystone Aircraft Company and the production facilities moved to Pennsylvania. Poor had been an accountant at Loening, while Swirbul and Schwendler worked as engineers and plant managers.

Central to the Grumman story is the man himself, Leroy Randle "Roy" Grumman. Born in Huntington, New York, in January 1895, Grumman's love of aviation dated back to his teenage years growing up on Long Island. Roy Grumman graduated from Cornell University in 1916 with a degree in Mechanical Engineering and then joined the Naval Reserve in June 1917. Grumman graduated flight school in September 1918 as Naval Aviator No. 1216 and was commissioned an ensign. He became a pilot instructor at NAS Pensacola, Florida, and later worked at the League Island Navy Yard near Philadelphia, where he worked as an acceptance test pilot for the Curtiss and Navy-built flying boats and as a project engineer for the Loening M-8 observation aircraft. Grumman so impressed the people at Loening, namely Grover Loening, that they offered him a job as an engineer in 1920. Grumman continued there until 1929.

The new Grumman Aircraft leased an 11,465-square-foot factory once used by the bankrupt Cox-Klemin Aircraft Corporation in Baldwin, New York, and officially opened for business on 1 January 1930. Grumman Aircraft took advantage of the high number of skilled workers who decided not to leave Long Island when Loening relocated to Pennsylvania. The company immediately began doing aircraft repair work and even ventured into aluminum truck body manufacturing while it attempted to get a foothold established in aircraft production with the Navy. Sure enough, Grumman Aircraft obtained a contract to produce amphibious floats, the Model A for the Vought O2U-4, and within 15 months of opening its doors, landed its first aircraft contract with the Navy for the FF-1, a high-performance two-seat fighter. Grumman also produced the F2F and F3F biplane fighters, which served with the Navy and Marine Corps during the mid-1930s and equipped all fleet squadrons beginning in 1936.

*Classic Grumman "meatball" logo used until the late 1970s.* (Northrop Grumman History Center)

Grumman Aircraft went on to produce two more amphibious (float) aircraft for the Navy and in 1936 received a contract for the XF4F-2 Wildcat monoplane of early World War II fame. That same year Grumman Aircraft purchased 120 acres in Bethpage, about 20 miles east of Baldwin, and began construction of a 65,000-square-foot plant. Grumman emerged as one of the leading producers of aircraft during the war, manufacturing a total of 17,573 aircraft at the Bethpage plant, including the famed F4F Wildcat (the Navy's first monoplane carrier-based fighter), F6F Hellcat, and F8F Bearcat fighters, and the TBF Avenger torpedo bomber. Grumman Aircraft contributions were so significant that it received the Navy's coveted "E" award for excellence in production achievement; with an additional six stars during the 1942 to 1945 time frame.

Grumman Aircraft's most famous postwar years undoubtedly came in the 1960s and 1970s with the design and production of the two-seat A-6 Intruder heavy attack aircraft and the supersonic swing-wing F-14 Tomcat fighter/interceptor. Both were exceptional aircraft. The A-6 saw significant action during the Vietnam War, retiring in late 1996, and the Tomcat, which joined the fleet in 1974, was just recently retired in 2006. The roles for both of these aircraft were taken over by the smaller, but more advanced multi-mission Boeing (formerly McDonnell Douglas) F/A-18 Hornet.

In 1969, Grumman Aircraft Engineering became Grumman Aerospace Corporation and would go on to be the leading supplier of naval carrier aircraft in the twentieth century. In 1994, Grumman was purchased by Northrop Corporation, and became Northrop Grumman. Today, Northrop Grumman ranks as the fourth largest defense contractor in the world, and it employs more than 122,000 people worldwide. The latest version of its 1960s-era E-2 Hawkeye Airborne Command aircraft, called the E-2C Hawkeye 2000, and C-2 Greyhound Carrier Onboard Delivery aircraft are still serving aboard American Navy carriers today. Grumman's long-flying EA-6B Prowler electronic countermeasures jet is just now being replaced with the new Boeing EA-18G Growler.

*Navy version of the Lockheed T-33 trainer, itself an outgrowth of the original P-80 Shooting Star, was designated the TV-2. It is seen here on a test flight over the mountains of Southern California near Lockheed's Burbank manufacturing facility.* (National Archives via Warren Hower)

(redesignated as VF-51) in November 1947. The Banshee, or "Banjo" as it was sometimes called, featured two Westinghouse J34-WE-22 3,000-lbf engines and was similar in appearance to the FH-1. The first Banshee rolled off the assembly line in August 1949 and deliveries began the following March made to VF-171 and VF-172 at NAS Cecil Field, Florida, as well as VX-3 at NAS Atlantic City. With four 20mm cannons and eight wing pylons each rated to carry 500 lbs, the Banshee served as a capable fighter-bomber. Production contracts followed in mid-1945 for the XF2D-1 Banshee (2 March) and the XFJ-1 Fury (28 May).

The Chance Vought offering did not fare as well. Powered by a single 3,000-lbf Westinghouse J34-WE-22, the Pirate first flew in October 1946. Called an "uninspiring design" by some observers, the Pirate looked more like a piston aircraft fitted with a turbojet. The XF6U was much less successful and its performance deemed unsatisfactory even with an added afterburner. As a result, it was canceled in 1950.

### Comparative Performance Data of First-Generation Navy Jet Fighters Versus Propeller-Driven F8F-2 Bearcat

|  | FJ-1 | F6U | FH-1 | F8F |
|---|---|---|---|---|
| Max. Speed (mph) | 510 | 478 | 479 | 455 |
| Std Rate of Climb (ft/min) | 5,660 | 8,060 | 4,230 | 6,300 |
| Range (miles) | 530 | 390 | 695 | 652 |
| Operational Ceiling (ft) | 38,000 | 46,300 | 41,100 | 40,800 |

Both the FJ-1 and the F2H were deployed with fleet squadrons and saw action in Korea. Moreover, the swept-wing version of the Fury continued in service into the 1960s.

### The Navy Acquires A Second Army Air Corps Jet Type

The Navy continued to test its three P-59A jets and in early 1945 acquired two P-80 Shooting Stars, which it designated as the TO-2s. These jets were sent

*An F2H-1 from VF-172 based at NAS Cecil Field, Florida, is seen here without wing tanks.* (U.S. Navy via Tailhook Association)

*At the outbreak of the Korean War, the F2H-1 was considered the East Coast fighter and the F9F-2 Panther the West Coast fighter. The Banshee saw its first carrier-based action on 23 August 1951 when launched with VF-172 as part of a Carrier Air Group Five strike from USS* Essex *(CV-9). Because of its good performance at high altitudes, the Banshee was used for long-range escort of USAF bombers.* (U.S. Navy via Tailhook Association)

to Patuxent River for flight test and evaluation work and to familiarize Navy pilots with basic jet operations. The first P-80A (BuNo 29667) arrived at NATC on 29 June 1945 and began trials the following week. In comparative air combat tests versus the Grumman F8F-1, the P-80A performed well. A second P-80A (BuNo 29688) arrived in December and was later modified with a tailhook and catapult fittings for carrier evaluations. After successful land-based tests in March 1946, which established an approach speed of 103 mph, the modified P-80A was sent to sea on 1 November aboard USS *Franklin D. Roosevelt* (CVB-42) for suitability trials. While two catapult launches, four free-deck takeoffs, and five arrested landings were successfully accomplished, the P-80A was nevertheless deemed unsuitable for carrier operations. These suitability tests put an end to any consideration of the proposed naval variant, the Lockheed P-80B (Navy designation FO-1), and solidified interest in the then-in-development McDonnell FD-1.

## Jet-Powered Night Fighter Contract

With its day fighter jet programs well underway, in early April 1945, BuAer issued a set of requirements calling for a jet-powered, long-range, all-weather, carrier-based night fighter. Although the development of radar for Navy aircraft had begun in 1941, it was not until early 1944 that the Navy actually developed a night fighter, the F4U-2.[xviii] According to the specifications, the design called for a "side-by-side, two-seat, carrier-based high-performance night fighter" capable of conducting night operations up to a range of 350 miles and able to attack both air and ground targets. Dimensions conducive to carrier stowage were specified as were minimum performance characteristics, including a top speed of at least 450 mph at sea level and a rate of climb of no less than 3,500 feet per second with full armament, fuel, and avionics. The design was also to include radar, which due to the complexities of the day required a dedicated radar operator as a second crewmember. The winning proposal was to be delivered to the Navy within 15 to 18 months of the contract.

Although the proposals were submitted to a dozen aerospace companies, only Douglas, Curtiss, Grumman, and Fleetwing responded by the 1 October deadline.[xix] Grumman's response consisted of a proposal called the Design Model G-75, on which work had commenced in September 1945.[xx] Measuring 46 feet, 0 inches long and having a wingspan of 64 feet, 2 inches, the G-75 was about the size of Grumman's F7F Tigercat, but was powered by four Westinghouse 24C 3,000-lbf turbojets arranged in pairs under each wing. The design looked quite capable on paper, touting performance of 608 mph at sea level and 575 mph at 40,000 feet, both well in excess of the government specifications. The G-75 also promised an impressive rate-of-climb of 11,400 feet-per-minute at sea level and a range of 388 miles. For its time, the G-75 represented a rather advanced design. The main landing gear, located in the wings, retracted into the space between the engine nacelles. The design further allowed for 1,530 gallons of fuel, carried in three self-sealing tanks located just aft of the cockpit.[xxi]

Douglas responded with its F3D Skyknight, a rather bulky design largely built around the extremely capable Westinghouse AN/APQ-35 multi-purpose radar. The F3D incorporated many of the features of the propeller-driven AD Skyraider, such as the barrel-like fuselage shape, conventional tail section, and large speed brakes. The engines, mounted in semi-buried pods, filled the lower center portion of the fuselage, with fuel cells installed directly above them. The F3D was about the same size as the G-75 proposal, measuring 45 feet, 5 inches long with a 50-foot, 0-inch wingspan, and was powered by two J34-WE-36 axial compressor jet engines, each generating 3,400 lbf.

Of the four responding proposals, the Navy selected two designs for development. According to a Navy report, the selection process was rather unconventional:

"Rather than evaluate each feature separately and then combine the evaluations in order to determine the most desirable aircraft, an alternative procedure was used whereby as many as possible of the aircraft were eliminated for such reasons as being too large for carrier operations, unsatisfactory carrier handling characteristics, inadequate high-speed performance, excessive time required for development, or unsatisfactory aerodynamic characteristics."[xxii]

An F3D from NATC reveals the stodgy lines of the aircraft. Notable are the large jet intakes below the cockpit and the aircraft's conventional tailplanes reminiscent of the Douglas AD Skyraider. The Skyknight used the same Westinghouse J42C engines intended for the Grumman XF9F-1. Although not as sleek as other contemporary jet fighters, the Skyknight was credited with making the first radar-directed kill of an enemy aircraft at night during the Korean War. (U.S. Navy via Tailhook Association)

This wood model shows a variation of the competing design under consideration by Grumman for the XF9F-1 night fighter. (Northrop Grumman History Center)

ensured developmental competition between the manufacturers to produce the best product.

The Navy and Grumman continued discussions and by June had mapped out a wind tunnel test program for the XF9F-1 as well as flight demonstration and design data requirements. Yet despite this progress, the Navy was concerned at what appeared to be a standstill in the Grumman program. In late May, it is reported that the aircraft project officer complained, "Airplane is now at a standstill and Grumman Company is expected to propose major modifications in view of F7F carrier operating difficulties."[xxiii] In 1946, problems with Grumman's F7F Tigercat carrier trials aboard USS *Shangri-La* (CVA-38) cast doubts on the suitability of the proposed XF9F-1. Although a propeller design, the F7F and the XF9F shared a similar airframe and undercarriage design. As a result of this development and other concerns about the engine configuration, the Navy issued a stop work order on 20 June.

Application of this methodology, the report continued, "resulted in the rejection of all designs save two—one Grumman and one Douglas." Preliminary negotiations continued with final proposals submitted by each company in March 1946.

On 3 April 1946, a Letter of Intent was issued to Douglas for its F3D design followed by issuance of a contract on 22 April to Grumman for production of two XF9F-1s. Grumman's prototypes were to be ready for flight 15, 16, and 17 months from the date of the Letter of Intent; essentially in June, July, and August 1947. Total prices for the two programs were set at $6,642,731.22 for the XF9F-1 and $7,108,789.92 for the XF3D-1. This dual contract offering was typical of the time, as the Navy desired to always have a fallback design. Moreover, having multiple designs

Rather than scrap the program and work through a new contract, however, BuAer issued a contract modification changing the Grumman proposal to cover a single-seat fighter, the XF9F-2, which Grumman had designated as the Model G-79. The amendment specified that two of the G-79 prototypes should be completed as XF9F-2s and powered by the imported Nene turbojet engine, and the third prototype, the XF9F-3, powered by the Allison J33 engine. As a precursor of things to come, the amendment also called for Grumman to submit plans for a swept-wing variant.

# GRUMMAN DESIGN 71

Although submitting a proposal responding to the Navy's September 1944 Request for Proposals, Grumman's proposal, Design 71, was the only one of the four rejected. Design 71 had a similar configuration (straight, low wings with wing-root intakes), as Chance Vought's V-340 proposal, which became the F6U, and was even powered by the same Westinghouse 24C (J34) turbojet. Aviation writer Tommy Thomason has commented that, "to buy

both would have been duplicative of configurations."[xxiv] Moreover, "[t]he Navy may therefore have decided that Grumman was currently busier than Vought with production and development of Navy propeller-driven fighters." Officially, however, the Navy told Grumman that the Design 71's wing was too thick and that it represented the slowest top speed of the four proposals. In the end, Design 71 had many similarities to what became the F9F-2.

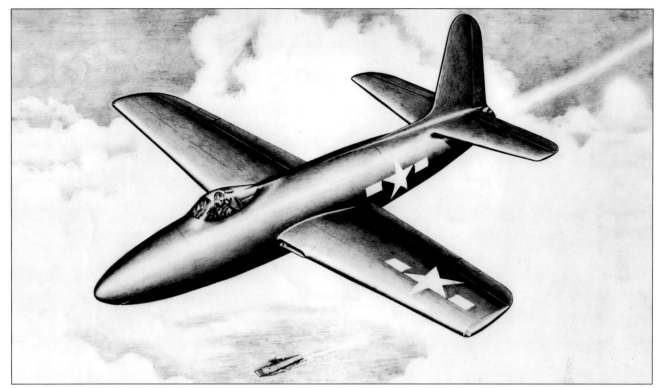

*This is an artist's depiction of the Design 71 jet fighter, which Grumman had proposed in response to the Navy's 1944 call for a day fighter. Grumman was the only manufacturer of the four submitting proposals not to be awarded a contract.* (Northrop Grumman Corporation via Tommy Thomason)

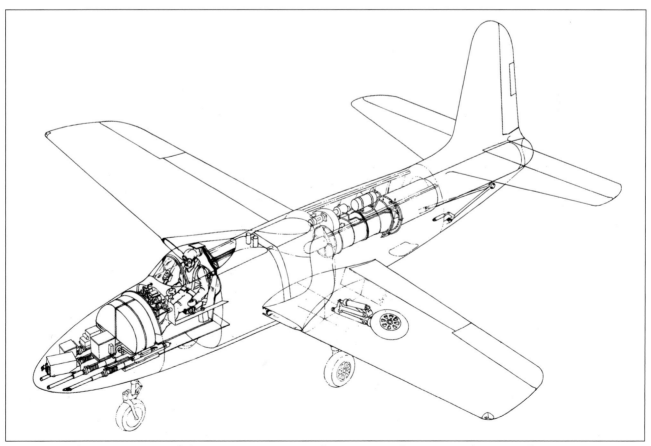

*The internal arrangement of the Design 71 is seen here, again showing similarity to the F9F-2. Note the location of the two fuel cells and the air intakes.* (Northrop Grumman Corporation via Tommy Thomason)

# CHAPTER TWO

# THE PANTHER IS BORN

*A stunning photograph of the F9F-2 Panther taken in early 1948 while flying over the snow-covered south shore of Long Island. Prototype had now been fitted with the Panther's trademark wingtip tanks.* (Northrop Grumman History Center)

M ost who have written on the topic acknowledge that Grumman was rather late coming into the jet age. During the World War II, Grumman busied itself with an impressive line of carrier-based fighters, namely the F4F Wildcat, F6F Hellcat, the late-war ground-based F7F Tigercat and F8F Bearcat, and the carried-based TBM Avenger torpedo bomber. Indeed, it seems clear that Grumman focused its efforts on meeting war demands and improving designs.[xxv] Moreover, Grumman corporate culture tended to be more conservative, and took a somewhat cautious approach to new technologies.

Nevertheless, there were several studies underway at Grumman examining the potential benefits of jet propulsion. In early 1944, Grumman fitted an XTBF-3 (BuNo 24141) with a 2,700-lbf Halford H-1B turbojet, which had been imported from Great Britain for use in the Curtiss XF15C composite fighter then under development. The H-1B was fitted in the fairing housing beneath the aircraft's R-2600 engine cowling grills, with the exhaust trailing beneath the center fuselage. Intakes for the turbojet were positioned on both sides of the forward fuselage. Ground testing began in November 1944, followed by test flights in December. The aircraft, dubbed *Fertile Myrtle*, marked Grumman's entry into the jet age, albeit with a composite effort.

Grumman also pursued other turbojet designs between July 1943 and November 1944.[xxvi] Although never reaching the proposal stage, engineers undertook preliminary work on a variety of combination designs, incorporating turbojets with piston engines. Design G-57 was initiated in July 1943 as an all-new design incorporating the Pratt & Whitney R-2800 engine and a small turbojet. One month later, work commenced on the G-61 design, a derivative of the F6F Hellcat with an auxiliary turbojet mounted in the tail section. Both were quickly abandoned in favor of the XF8F-1. In July 1944, designers proposed a variant of the F7F-2, called the G-67, which featured a small auxiliary turbojet mounted aft of each piston engine. Two single-seat, single-jet proposals were also forwarded to BuAer, the G-63 and the G-71, which had begun in August 1943 and November 1944, and the G-68, which was terminated almost as quickly as the program commenced in June 1944. BuAer pursued neither the G-67 nor the two single-engine designs.

As mentioned earlier, Grumman's most significant early jet offering came by way of the XF9F-1 jet-powered night fighter proposal.[xxvii] Work on the XF9F-1 began in September 1945 following the BuAer Request for Proposal (RFP) for a two-seat, jet-powered, carried-based night fighter. Although four companies had responded to the RFP, the Douglas (F3D) and Grumman designs were selected. On 22 April 1946, BuAer placed an order for two XF9F prototypes, as a fallback should the Douglas design, ordered eight days prior, not meet expectations. However, that program was all but terminated by late June, due to carrier suitability problems

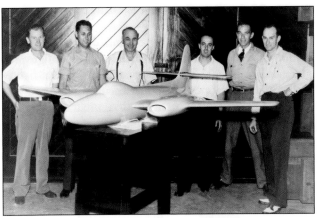

*Grumman engineers gather around a wood model of the Design 79-C offering. The model strongly resembled the Panther, except for its two wing-mounted Rolls-Royce Derwent VI engines.* (Northrop Grumman History Center)

experienced by Grumman with the F7F Tigercat, which was similar in design to the XF9F-1.

In early 1946, studies were also underway at Grumman on the proposed G-79 design, a single-seat, single-jet day fighter, partly in response to BuAer's 1944 industry RFP calling for a carrier-based day fighter to supersede the first generation FH-1 and FJ-1, which were already inferior as compared to other land-based jet fighters. Grumman began informal discussions with the Navy in June 1946 and a formal proposal followed on 30 August. Initially, Design 79 was to be powered by a centrifugal-flow 3,750- to 4,000-lbf turbojet, such as the Allison J33 or General Electric J35, to be mounted in-line with a single rear exhaust, or two wing-mounted, 3,000-lbf Westinghouse J34 axial flow turbojets.

It was about this same time, however, that concerns were mounting, both within the government and Grumman, over the XF9F-1 design. Rather than cancel the XF9F-1 contract altogether, BuAer amended the contract on 9 October 1946, both canceling the XF9F-1 development and ordering three of the XF9F-2 single-seat, single-engine designs (BuNos 122475 through 122477), plus a static-test airframe and design data supporting a swept-wing version and three spare engines. Initially, the Navy, led by Head of Fighter Design, Capt. A. B. Metsger, wanted at least one of the F9F prototypes to be a swept-wing, and indeed this was reflected in the recommendations of the 2 July BuAer/Grumman conference, which had asked for two straight-winged prototypes and one swept-wing design to serve as a prototype for the ultimate high-performance interceptor. Apparently Capt. Metsger viewed the straight-winged Panther as an interim fighter. However, Grumman declined and the Navy agreed to accept preliminary swept-wing design studies. Apparently, the development of one swept-wing prototype would have added another $1 million to the contract.

largest of the four studies, possessing a 42-foot, 5-inch wingspan and measuring 40 feet, 0 inches in length. Wing area, at 362 square feet, also trumped all others. Study 79D was powered by a single Rolls-Royce Nene engine and presented the best performance numbers of the four, promising, on paper, a top speed of 598 mph at sea level and a rate of climb of 10,550 feet per minute at sea level. Grumman argued hard for the Study 79C design, citing its ease of maintenance and the added reliability of two engines for over-ocean flight. Moreover, it did not believe that the Nene-powered Study 79D could be ready within the required two years. The two composite designs were never seriously considered, as it was by then recognized that the future was in jets rather than a combined propulsion.

The Navy favored Study 79D, although with some modifications, and it was formally accepted in June 1946. Despite the lack of any degree of similarity to the XF9F-1, the Navy designated Design 79D the XF9F-2. Shortly thereafter, Grumman named the aircraft the Panther, adhering to its tradition of naming its naval fighters after members of the cat family. Grumman immediately began work on the mockup and prototypes, which were slated to fly in late 1947. Aerodynamic tests commenced in the fall of 1946, with a 1/16-scale model being constructed and sent to the Massachusetts Institute of Technology's wind tunnels. As the program proposal stated, the tests were "to determine longitudinal, directional, and lateral stability and control, stalling characteristics, and C/L max, and will serve to disclose and correct any major faults in the basic airplane design."[xxix]

### Engine Selection

Grumman Aircraft was known as a company with a conservative design philosophy and that applied equally to its use of powerplants. As Corky Meyer explained in his book on the Panther:

"Grumman's policy in selecting powerplants for every new model was to use the very latest squadron reliable engine currently in production. The management didn't want new-engine problems associated with experimental airplanes to complicate the normal gestation trials of new airframe development programs, at least until the prototype machine had been thoroughly tested."[xxx]

According to Meyer, this approach, which was endorsed by the company's top management (all of whom were former test pilots), "ensured that an early prototype aircraft would have the greatest chance of survival and avoid the engine failures which had caused major schedule delays in several important fighter programs."[xxxi]

With this philosophy governing, Grumman's engineers began searching for the ideal jet engine to power their new programs. As Meyer noted, several of the Grumman test pilots had flown and evaluated the Bell YP-59, with its twin 1,650-lbf GE J31-GE-3 turbojet

engines, and were likewise familiar with other models. John Karanik, head of Grumman's propulsion department, had also studied several of the leading American jet engines of the time, including the Westinghouse J34, General Electric's I-40 (later the J35), and Allison's J33. However, none of these seemed to meet Grumman's demands. Karanik then turned his attention to British engines and visited Rolls-Royce, where he witnessed firsthand the Halford, Derwent, and Nene turbojet engines. Of all the engines evaluated, Karanik was most impressed with the Nene's power and record of trouble-free ground and flight testing.

When Design 79D was first proposed to the Navy, at least three engines were being considered, ranging from the Allison J33 (formerly the I-40), essentially an enlarged version of the Rolls-Royce Derwent used by

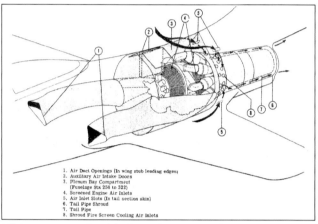

1. Air Duct Openings (In wing stub leading edges)
2. Auxiliary Air Intake Doors
3. Plenum Bay Compartment (Fuselage Sta 258 to 322)
4. Screened Engine Air Inlets
5. Air Inlet Slots (In tail section skin)
6. Tail Pipe Shroud
7. Tail Pipe
8. Shroud Fire Screen Cooling Air Inlets

**This cutaway highlights the air-intake system used by the Panther. The intakes were positioned at the wing stub and brought air into the combustion chamber.** (Flight Manual for the F9F-2 and F9F-3 Airplane)

**The Panther was a maintenance crewman's dream. The aircraft's aft fuselage completely separated to allow easy access to the Pratt & Whitney J42 engine and also enabled quick replacement, when necessary. The J42-P-4 (and later uprated -6 version) powered the XF9F-2 and production models.** (Northrop Grumman History Center)

*The Panther's leading-edge slats, a novel design characteristic for the day, can be seen in this photo of the mockup.* (Northrop Grumman History Center)

the P-80 Shooting Star, to the General Electric J35, which powered the FJ-1 Fury, to Westinghouse's J34 (formerly known as the 24C), which powered the F2H Banshee and F3D Skyknight. As noted earlier, the Navy considered using two J35s mounted in wing nacelles.

*Grumman prepared a full-size wood mockup for the January 1947 Navy inspections. The design was approved by the Navy with minor changes.* (Northrop Grumman History Center)

During mid-summer 1946, and based on Karanik's visit to Great Britain, Grumman suggested using the 5,000-lbf Rolls-Royce Nene centrifugal-flow turbojet engine. The new fledgling Taylor Turbine Corporation had recently obtained a license to build the Nene in the United States, having signed an agreement on 8 August. At the time of the October contract amendment and because of the uncertainty still surrounding the actual engine for the Design 79, the Navy requested that two of the XF9F prototypes, designated as the XF9F-2 (BuNos 122475 and 122477), be built using the imported Nene engine and that one prototype, designated as the XF9F-3 (BuNo 122476), be fitted with the less-powerful Allison J33.

The Navy, however, was concerned that Taylor, given its recent incorporation and small size, would not be able to keep up with production demands. As a result, the Navy urged transfer of the license to Pratt & Whitney, which had established itself during the war years with its production of piston engines. The Navy was certainly aware of the potential of the Nene engine. On 30 June 1946, two examples were obtained for testing

*This profile view of the XF9F-2 mockup shows the familiar Panther lines, and even shows such Navy-oriented detail as the open canopy, just the way the aircraft would be flown for carrier launches and arrested landings.* (Northrop Grumman History Center)

*A three-quarter rear view highlights the tall tail section design needed for good lateral stability. The Panther's vertical stabilizer stood 11 feet, 4 inches; the horizontal stabilizer had a span of 17 feet, 2½ inches.* (Northrop Grumman History Center)

by the Naval Air Materiel Command at its Aeronautical Engine Laboratory in Philadelphia. Negotiations between Pratt & Whitney and Rolls-Royce took place in

*The first XF9F-2 prototype (BuNo 122475) sits on the tarmac at Bethpage in late 1947 during company test flights.* (Northrop Grumman History Center)

*The Allison J33-A-8 powered the XF9F-3 and production F9F-3 models. The J33 was less powerful than the J42 and most F9F-3s were re-engined with the Pratt & Whitney model.* (Northrop Grumman History Center)

early 1947, which resulted in a transfer of the license from Taylor to Pratt & Whitney.

Plans were given to Pratt & Whitney in mid-July and work immediately began on what had been now redesignated as the J42 engine. Pratt & Whitney made the transition rather quickly, despite difficulties in converting British blueprints to American engineering standards and the need to redesign the fuel pump to use gasoline rather than kerosene, as used by the British. Even with Pratt & Whitney's successes, it was apparent that the J42 would not be ready for the XF9F-2 flight testing planned for late fall.[xxxii] To solve this shortcoming, Taylor provided six of its imported Rolls-Royce Nene engines, designated as the J42-TT-2, for prototype testing. It was not until 6 March 1948 that Pratt & Whitney first ran an experimental J42 and September before the first production engine was available. The 150-hr qualification test, which lasted seven months, confirmed the ratings of 5,000 lbf static and 5,750 lbf with water injection. A J42-P-6 was flown in the first production F9F-2 (BuNo 122560) on 24 November 1948. A total of 1,139 J42-P engines were ultimately produced under the -4, -6, and -8 designations.

The XF9F-3 was ordered with the Allison J33-A-23 engine as an alternative and back up engine program in the event the Nene modifications experienced delays. The J33 produced 4,600 lbf and had already been in use with the U.S. Air Force's P-80 program. General Electric designed the J33, but because it could not keep up with production demands, it was licensed to the Allison Division of General Motors, which produced the J33-A-23 used by the Panther. The -23 provided 4,600 lbf static and 5,400 lbf with water injection.

Further revisions of Design 79D took place throughout the summer and fall of 1946, with major changes being the relocation of the cockpit further aft, extension of the exhaust further aft, and a redesign of the tail surfaces.

*The XF9F-2 prototype (BuNo 122475) sits on the ramp at Grumman's plant in Bethpage with a tow bar affixed to its nose gear prior to its third flight. Note the small, black "panther" insignia on the nose.* (Northrop Grumman History Center)

The XF9F-2/XF9F-3 mockup inspection took place in January and February 1947, and the design was approved with minor changes. Actual construction of the two XF9F-2s began shortly thereafter, and by mid-1947, as noted in the discussion of the jet engines, all engine issues were resolved.

## Core Panther Specifications

Although explained in more detail in subsequent chapters, the basic Panther configuration was that of a "single seat, folding mid-wing high performance day fighter, equipped with tricycle landing gear and powered by turbo jet engines."[xxxiii] Innovative for its day, the Panther contained a pressurized, air-conditioned cockpit, self-sealing fuel tanks, a quick-release, one-piece, bubble canopy, and was designed with easily removable nose and tail sections, which permitted quick access to the armaments (nose) and engine (tail). The Panther wing also featured a new design, a forward-sliding leading-edge flap known as the "droop snoot," which provided added lift on landing and takeoff. The aircraft featured hydraulically folding wings, which folded upward to 90 degrees. The folding wings were later modified to 62 degrees on production aircraft.[xxxiv]

### Approximate Overall F9F Dimensions

| | |
|---|---|
| Wing Span | 38 feet, 0 inches |
| Span, Wings Folded | 23 feet, 5 inches |
| Stabilizer Span | 17 feet, 2½ inches |
| Length | 37 feet, 10 inches |
| Height, Tail | 11 feet, 4 inches |
| Height, Wings Folded | 16 feet, 10 inches |
| Wing Area | 250 square feet |

The aircraft's gross weight varied from an empty weight of 7,304 pounds to a maximum of 12,420 pounds, depending on the load carried. Total fuel (prior to wingtip tank installation) was listed at 683 gallons.

*Gear coming up into the wells, the XF9F-2 takes to the air for its maiden flight on 21 November 1947. Famed Grumman test pilot Corwin "Corky" Meyer was at the controls that day, and wound up landing the new jet at the larger Idlewild Airport nearby rather than chance an overrun of the shorter prop-era runways at Bethpage.* (Northrop Grumman History Center)

*This view of the gleaming bare-metal XF9F-2 prototype gives a good indication of the narrow track of the airplane's main landing gear.* (Northrop Grumman History Center)

*The other feature of the Panther design that greatly reduced maintenance time was the sliding nose section, which allowed easy access to the armament and electronics. This would later prove to be a bonus when the Navy redesigned the Panther's nose to accommodate photographic equipment for the F9F-2P. Odd-looking device above the aircraft's tail section is the foam spray boom of an airport CARDOX fire truck parked behind the airplane.* (Northrop Grumman History Center)

*Corky Meyer poses for an air-to-air photo during the airplane's first flight. Notice the prominent zero-degree angle of incidence as well as heavy cloud cover that day.* (Northrop Grumman History Center)

*Now sporting a snazzy black-panther nose art insignia, an instrumented XF9F-2 awaits flight testing at Grumman's Bethpage plant. Note data booms mounted on both the nose and tailfin of the airplane.* (Northrop Grumman History Center)

### First Flight and Flight Testing

The first prototype (BuNo 122475) began engine ground running tests in October 1947. On 21 November 1947, Grumman test pilot Corwin "Corky" Meyer made the first flight of the Panther. A flight had been planned for a week earlier, but the aircraft had been damaged after getting stuck in the mud when Meyer tried to cross a muddy area between the runways.[xxxv] Meyer tried to dislodge the Panther by applying full power, but it would not budge. A tow truck had to be called to remove the XF9F-2, but in the process, damaged the nose gear. The aircraft spent part of the next week in the plant undergoing repairs and pre-flight checks.

Meyer's initial flight departed from Bethpage's 5,000-foot runway and landed at New York

*Test pilot Corky Meyer inspects the XF9F-2 one day prior to its first flight on 21 November 1947.* (Northrop Grumman History Center)

*The second XF9F-2 prototype, BuNo 122477, is shown here on the runway at Bethpage, with instrumentation affixed to the nose and the black-panther insignia.* (Northrop Grumman History Center)

*An excellent view of a highly polished XF9F-3 in flight sometime during 1948, with wingtip tanks installed.* (Northrop Grumman History Center)

*This picture shows the XF9F-3 at Bethpage in an odd configuration with one wing folded and the other in its proper inflight position. Note right aileron fully deflected upward.* (Northrop Grumman History Center)

*This excellent photograph of a Marine Corps Panther on final approach clearly shows its arresting hook ready to catch a wire. The LSO can be seen in the background watching the landing.* (National Archives)

International Airport, known as Idlewild, some 40 miles to the west. (That airport later became John F. Kennedy International Airport.) Idlewild's runway measured 8,000 feet long and provided the additional room needed in the event the Panther proved long in its rollout. According to Meyer, the Navy had insisted on using the longer runway because Grumman had declined the Navy's invitation to ship the Panther to the Naval Air Test Center at Patuxent River, Maryland, which also had a long runway. Meyer was uneasy with the Navy's mandate, as it meant he had to fly an untested aircraft over the densely populated Long Island suburbs.

Meyer said that the flight test was flown in the worst weather he'd ever encountered for a first flight. In the face of gathering clouds and a 9,000-foot ceiling, he took off from Bethpage and headed south. During the 30-minute flight, Meyer performed a variety of tests, including simulated stalls, which he described as "very gentle …with no wing dropping."[xxxvi] Based on these stall tests, he quickly concluded that the Panther would not require the longer runway prescribed by the Navy and that it would have easily landed on Bethpage's 5,000-foot runways. In fact, Meyer radioed back to Bethpage and asked permission to return to the plant, but was overruled by management.

Meyer's return flight encountered rain and he just managed to beat an incoming rainstorm.[xxxvii] During the

flight, Meyer noticed that he had inadvertently reached 450-mph airspeed, some 200 mph over the maximum limit he had been given for the flight. He quickly engaged his speed brakes and went to idle power, bringing the aircraft's speed back within limits. After landing, Meyer realized that he had inadvertently completed more than 50 percent of the structural flight envelope in just seven minutes—and under instrument conditions, at that!

The second XF9F-2 (BuNo 122477) flew a few days later on 26 November. Neither prototype was fitted with the planned armament (four 20mm cannons), or an operating ejection seat. Company test flights during the remainder of 1947 were generally uneventful. The aircraft was fully cleared for 650 mph and 7-g flight. Meyer was interviewed in *Aero Digest* in mid-1948 concerning his impressions of the Panther's handling qualities.

"I asked him what he thought of the F9F, and he just grinned." "It's by all odds the best thing we have to date. Simple to start—flip three switches, touch a fourth, wait about 30 seconds and off you go. Climb? It gets to 10,000 feet in a little over a minute, and it's *very* maneuverable."[xxxviii]

"How about top speed and range?" the reporter asked Meyer. "Well, [the] Navy only lets us say it's in the 600-mph class; but I can tell you it really does that and better, and they are very chary about range figures. The production jobs will have wingtip tanks and we expected

The three prototype aircraft featured wings that folded upward to a full 90-degree angle. This design feature was standard for carrier-based Navy aircraft, and was intended to allow more space-efficient carrier deck storage. (Northrop Grumman History Center)

One of the prototypes in a hangar at Grumman in mid-February 1948 with the new wingtip tanks installed. The tanks were added following comments by the Navy during initial flight tests that the Panther had insufficient range. Note data boom affixed to the left wingtip tank shown here. (Northrop Grumman History Center)

An operational photorecon F9F-5P is shown here with its wings folded in an aircraft carrier hangar bay. The angle had to be reduced from 90 degrees, as found on the prototype aircraft, to provide clearance for the wingtip tanks. (Northrop Grumman History Center)

to get a range comparable with our piston-engined fighters during the war."[xxxix]

The Panther flight test program began in early 1948 using the two XF9F-2s—the XF9F-3 did not make its first flight until 16 August 1948. Test flights by Grumman and the Navy revealed two significant problems with the aircraft, namely, that it laterally snaked at all speeds, especially at reduced-fuel states and that it was unstable longitudinally at low speeds, particularly during landings. The former condition was especially significant in that oscillations hampered effective weapons targeting.

Several attempts were made to cure the problem, including modifications to the fairing around the tailpipe and under the fin, without real progress. The true fix came through the recognition that fuel was sloshing around in the round-bottomed fuselage fuel tanks. Two levels of 6-inch, horizontal baffles were installed around the inside of the tanks, which resolved the problem temporarily. However, it was soon discovered that the baffles and fasteners were not strong enough to combat the swishing fuel. More secure fasteners were added, which permanently resolved the problem. The instability issue was corrected through modifications to the tail surface controls, namely, increasing the area of the fin and rudder.

One of the more significant Navy evaluations took place in early 1948 by Capt. Fred Trapnell, the Navy's lead test pilot. Trapnell performed a three-day evaluation, including several test flights, and in his final report, concluded that the aircraft's ailerons, which were hydraulically boosted (at a 33:1 ratio), required too much exertion when operated manually in the event of a hydraulic failure. Trapnell also questioned the Panther's range, commenting that it was insufficient. Grumman redesigned the aileron control, creating a system that provided a double-mechanical advantage when operated

One of the prototypes undergoes inspection at Grumman's Bethpage plant. The aft section and a portion of the canopy have been removed for display purposes. Judging from the heavy coats being worn by personnel, this photo must have been taken in early 1948, as there are no instruments mounted on the nose and the panther insignia has yet to be applied. (Northrop Grumman History Center)

# CORWIN "CORKY" MEYER

Few individuals are more associated with the Panther than Corwin "Corky" Meyer, Grumman's project pilot for some of the most famous fighters in naval aviation. Meyer, who was not a military pilot, joined Grumman in 1942 as an experimental test pilot and progressed to the position of project pilot for the F6F Hellcat, F7F Tigercat, F8F Bearcat, F9F Panther, F10 Jaguar, F11 Tiger, and the Super Tiger. Meyer also holds the distinction of becoming the first civilian to qualify aboard a United States Navy aircraft carrier, having accomplished the feat while flying an F9F Cougar with VF-61 aboard USS *Lake Champlain* (CVA-39) in 1954. Meyer became the Director of Delivery of Aircraft in 1965 and four years later assumed the position of Vice President of Manufacturing Operations and Quality Control. In 1974, Meyer became President and CEO of Grumman American, which was a commercial subsidiary. He retired from Grumman in 1978.

*This illustrates the nose-shredding problem that Navy pilots experienced during the early months of the Korean War, which was caused by a build-up of gun gas that subsequently exploded. Grumman solved the problem by venting the nose cone and by adding a small see-through window so the pilot could confirm that the nose lock mechanism was indeed in the secure position. It was a tacit testimony to the Panther's airworthiness that the aircraft could still be flown in this situation.* (Naval Aviation Museum)

*Corwin "Corky" Meyer was the lead Grumman test pilot for the XF9F-2/-3 program and participated in much of the flight test evaluation. He has authored several books on the F9F, including* Corky Meyer's Flight Journal *(published by Specialty Press).* (Northrop Grumman History Center)

*One of the prototypes with wings folded, and painted in Navy dark blue fleet colors prior to test work at NATC.* (Northrop Grumman History Center)

*Two Marine Corps F9F-2 Panthers sit on the catapult of a Midway-class aircraft carrier awaiting launch. Note the modest jet blast deflector shown in its raised position behind the aircraft on the catapult, and the deck crewman directing the second airplane to taxi to the starboard cat.* (Naval Aviation Museum)

Following the successful flight tests, two separate production contracts were issued, the first for 9 F9F-2s and 21 F9F-3s and the second for 38 F9F-2s and 33 F9F-3s. In the end, some 563 F9F-2s and 54 F9F-3s were built.[xlii] Three additional F9F-2s had been planned, but were converted on the line to serve as the XF9F-4 (BuNo 123084), XF9F-5 (BuNo 123085), and XF9F-4/-5 static (BuNo 123086) airframes. As noted earlier, the general configuration was of a single-seat, mid-wing high-performance jet day fighter. Production F9F-2s were externally identical to the XF9F-2, with the exception of the added wingtip tanks. Moreover, they were considerably heavier in all configurations, largely due to the added fuel capacity, installation of the Martin-Baker ejection seat, and the addition of the four 20mm cannons and ammunition.

This chapter takes a look into the actual systems of the early Panther, many of which were considered state of the art for the time, 1948, and many of which further formed the foundation of the systems found in current aircraft of the day. What follows below covers both the F9F-2 and F9F-3; the sole difference between the two being the powerplant and supporting systems. In all other respects, the two were identical.

## Basic Fuselage Design

The Panther presented a rather sleek design and featured a three-piece aluminum fuselage that permitted easy removal of nose cone and tail section. The nose section could be pulled forward on rails, or quickly removed for full access to the cannons or, in photoreconnaissance

*An F9F-2 (BuNo 127561) is ready to be rolled off the production line. Here, workers prepare the airplane for final systems tests before rolling the jet to the paint shop. Denoting the fact that the airplane's fuel system will be pressure checked, placard resting against the nosewheel says "Warning—This Ship Gassed."* (Northrop Grumman History Center)

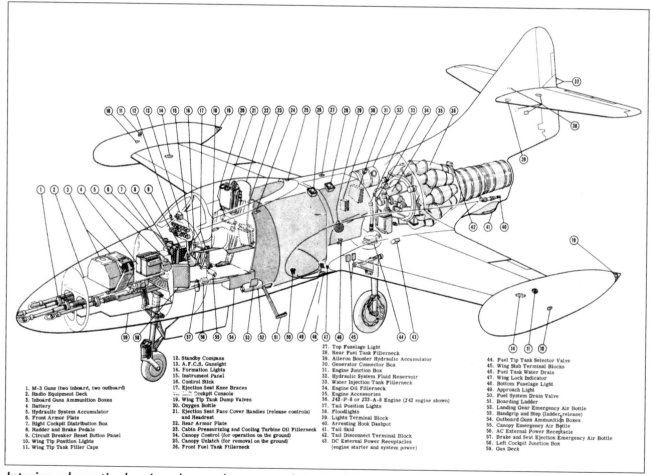

1. M-3 Guns (two inboard, two outboard)
2. Radio Equipment Deck
3. Inboard Guns Ammunition Boxes
4. Battery
5. Hydraulic System Accumulator
6. Front Armor Plate
7. Right Cockpit Distribution Box
8. Rudder and Brake Pedals
9. Circuit Breaker Reset Button Panel
10. Wing Tip Position Lights
11. Wing Tip Tank Filler Caps
12. Standby Compass
13. A.F.C.S. Gunsight
14. Formation Lights
15. Instrument Panel
16. Control Stick
17. Ejection Seat Knee Braces
18. Left Cockpit Console
19. Wing Tip Tank Dump Valves
20. Oxygen Bottle
21. Ejection Seat Face Cover Handles (release controls) and Headrest
22. Rear Armor Plate
23. Cabin Pressurizing and Cooling Turbine Oil Fillerneck
24. Canopy Control (for operation on the ground)
25. Canopy Unlatch (for removal on the ground)
26. Front Fuel Tank Fillerneck
27. Top Fuselage Light
28. Rear Fuel Tank Fillerneck
29. Aileron Booster Hydraulic Accumulator
30. Generator Connector Box
31. Engine Junction Box
32. Hydraulic System Fluid Reservoir
33. Water Injection Tank Fillerneck
34. Engine Oil Fillerneck
35. Engine Accessories
36. J42-P-8 or J33-A-8 Engine (J42 engine shown)
37. Tail Position Lights
38. Floodlights
39. Lights Terminal Block
40. Arresting Hook Dashpot
41. Tail Skid
42. Tail Disconnect Terminal Block
43. DC External Power Receptacles (engine starter and system power)
44. Fuel Tip Tank Selector Valve
45. Wing Stub Terminal Blocks
46. Fuel Tank Water Drain
47. Wing Lock Indicator
48. Bottom Fuselage Light
49. Approach Light
50. Fuel System Drain Valve
51. Boarding Ladder
52. Landing Gear Emergency Air Bottle
53. Handgrip and Step (ladder, release)
54. Outboard Guns Ammunition Boxes
55. Canopy Emergency Air Bottle
56. AC External Power Receptacle
57. Brake and Seat Ejection Emergency Air Bottle
58. Left Cockpit Junction Box
59. Gun Deck

*Interior schematic drawing shows placement of the Panther's armament, cockpit, fuel tanks, and powerplant relative to the overall airframe structure.* (Northrop Grumman History Center)

*The speed brakes and pilot entry steps are visible in this photograph. Notice the white lines directing the pilot to the steps. This self-contained boarding method was a standard feature on carrier-based Navy aircraft since Air Force-type boarding ladders would become serious safety hazards if they were ever dropped and blown around a carrier deck by jet blasts.* (Jim Sullivan Collection)

models, the cameras and film. This method allowed deck crews to work on the cannons, load the magazines, or work on the radio gear from deck or ground level. Likewise, the Panther's aft section, separated at section 299, exposed the aft portion of the turbojet engine and allowed maintenance crews access to a majority of the systems. Both were welcomed design innovations from a maintenance standpoint and were the principal reason for the reduction in maintenance man-hours required to keep the Panther flying.

### Overall F9F-2/F9F-3 Dimensions

| | |
|---|---|
| Wing Span | 38 feet, 0 inches |
| Span, Wings Folded | 23 feet, 5 inches |
| Span Stabilizer | 17 feet, 2½ inches |
| Length | 37 feet, 10 inches |
| Height, Tail | 11 feet, 4 inches |
| Height, Wings Folded | 16 feet, 10 inches |
| Wing Area | 250 square feet |

Gross weight varied between 9,800 and 15,700 pounds, depending on loads carried.

### Cockpit

Compared to other jet fighters of the day, the Panther's cockpit was considered rather spacious. The flight instrumentation was typical of the day, with fuel and oil pressure indicators, altimeters, accelerometer, main and stand-by compasses, a tachometer, fuel quantity indicator, a turn-and-bank indicator, and various temperature indicators for the engine and tailpipe. The arresting hook lever was located at the lower left side. The cockpit featured a Grumman-designed ejection seat and used traditional center stick and rudder controls and a left-hand console-mounted throttle. The flight control stick had a gun trigger located on the stick grip and in later production aircraft, an elevator tab control switch on the thumb portion. A rocket-bomb switch was later added to the left side of the stick as part of the F9F-2B modifications. A radio switch and speed brake switch were located on the throttle.

*Having input from pilots is invaluable for cockpit design. Here, a Grumman engineer discusses F9F cockpit layout with a Naval Aviator. White rope hanging to the right in foreground is a yaw string used to show proper attitude orientation inflight.* (Northrop Grumman Historical Center)

The Panther's instrument panel was state of the art for the late 1940s, and was considered fairly straightforward by pilots. (Northrop Grumman History Center)

## Flight Control Systems

Despite strong suggestions from the Navy during the negotiations stage that a swept-wing design be considered, the Panther was a straight-wing design. Wingspan, including the permanently installed wingtip tanks, measured 37 feet, 10 inches and wing surfaces provided total area of 250 square feet. The wings were a symmetrical section, 12 degrees thick at the 40-degree chord, and mounted at 0-degree angle of incidence. The wings folded upward hydraulically to an angle of 62 degrees for storage on the carrier deck and hangar bay. The XF9F-2 and -3 featured a full 90-degree wing fold, similar to other carrier-based jets of the era.

The flight control system consisted of conventional ailerons, elevators, a rudder, and trim tabs (manual at first), plus wing flaps and leading edge flaps, all mechanically connected to the stick and rudder via a system of cables and pulleys. The ailerons and elevators were controlled by the stick and operated by a push-pull cable and linkage rod, and a hydraulically operated booster unit for the ailerons. The ailerons were of all-metal construction and extended inboard from the wingtips about 25 percent of the semi-span. Together, they comprised a total of 18.44 square feet. Stemming from the Navy's comments during flight tests, an emergency aileron control was also provided in the event of hydraulic failure, which activated when booster pressure dropped below 400 psi. In such a situation, a spring would retract the aileron control, shortening the lever arm, and thus doubling the mechanical advantage of the control linkage.

Conventional foot pedals provided rudder control. The pedals were adjustable fore and aft up to 9 inches and also served as toe brakes when the Panther was on the ground. The rudder deflected 25 degrees each direction. Trim tabs were located on the left aileron and rudder and were controlled from the cockpit by handwheels and gearboxes. This was modified on aircraft 125083 and subsequent aircraft with the addition of a three-position electrical switch on the control stick—"nose down," "off," and "nose up." The trim tabs had a +/- 5-degree deflection. Former Panther pilot Walter Spangenberg, who flew the F9F-2 as a Lieutenant (j.g.) with VF-91, commented on this modification:

"The early Panthers had a handwheel and cable arrangement, which never caused any comment or problem as far as I know. The later aircraft had an electric elevator trim button on the control stick, which did cause problems in working air-to-ground, as with guns, bombs,

The left-hand console, which was stepped-up aft-to-forward, contained the throttle, oxygen controls, wing flap controls, speed brake control on the throttle, and many of the engine and fuel controls. The right-hand console contained much of the electrical and communications gear, as well as the wing-lock mechanism. The overall layout remained largely the same over the entire production run, although slight modifications were made beginning with aircraft 123465, which made the instruments more readable (generally of larger print). Of interest, the compass included in the redesign featured a swept-wing aircraft overlay.

An employee works on the relatively simple but well-engineered wing fold mechanism as this Panther moves down the production line. (Northrop Grumman History Center)

and rockets. We normally used a 45-degree dive angle and the electric elevator trim did not work fast enough to keep up with the aircraft acceleration in the dive, so the pilot would have to pre-trim the nose-down early in the dive, and then correct as he could during the dive."[xliii]

"This," Spangenberg added, "was a distraction we did not need."

The outboard wing flaps were positioned on the inner aspect of the rear of each wing and could be positioned in an "up," "landing," or "takeoff" position. These flaps were hinged at the 70 percent chord point and provided 54.3 square feet of lift surface. Two smaller inboard flaps were located under the fuselage. For take-off position, the inboard flap deflected 45 degrees, the outboard flap deflected 40 degrees, and the leading edge deflected 19 degrees. In the landing position, a limit switch held the inboard flaps at 19 degrees deflection to prevent damage caused by insufficient deck clearance when the landing gear fully compressed on impact. The leading-edge flaps (called a "droop snoot") helped adapt the thin, high-speed wing design to permit carrier landings and takeoffs by providing increased lift. On aircraft 125083 and beyond, a portion of the trailing edge of each outboard flap was deflected automatically when the flaps were lowered to provide additional clearance for the external stores on the inboard bomb racks.

An F9F-2 (BuNo 123451) flies chase for the first production F9F-3 (BuNo 122560). Thin white "T" shape just aft of the national insignia are guidelines for the pilot's feet to help locate the fold-in steps leading up to the airplane's cockpit. (Northrop Grumman History Center)

### Flight Speed Limitations

| | |
|---|---|
| Landing Gear, Normal Extension | 230 knots IAS |
| Landing Flaps | 130 knots IAS |
| Canopy (closed above) | 200 knots IAS |
| Dive Brakes | No Limitations |

Two-speed "Swiss cheese" speed brakes were located just aft of the nose gear and could be positioned at any angle up to 75 degrees of deflection. Cleverly, an unpainted portion of the inboard section of the left wingtip tank surface served as a mirror enabling the pilot to check the position of the speed brake as well as confirm the status of his nose gear.

### Powerplant, Electrical and Hydraulic Systems

Although the F9F-2 and F9F-3 used different turbojet engines, the two powerplants nevertheless shared many common features. The F9F-2 utilized an Americanized version of the Rolls-Royce Nene engine, designated as the J42-P while the F9F-3 was powered by the Allison J33 turbojet. Both were non-afterburning, continuous-flow, dual-entry centrifugal compressor-driven turbojets. The J42 utilized nine combustion chambers and delivered air under a pressure ratio of 4.3:1 at sea level static conditions.

The J33 was a 14 chamber centrifugal compressor that used a single-stage turbine. Regardless of the engine, combustion air for the Panther's jet engines was taken in through triangular duct openings in the wing stub leading edges. The wing roots were thickened to accommodate the ducts. Two hinged "blow-in" doors at the fuselage spine (just forward of the vertical stabilizer) were set to open automatically to provide additional air during takeoff and low-speed flight conditions.

Both engines featured a water injection system that provided added thrust, giving the J42 5,750 lbf and the J33 5,400 lbf. The J42-P water injection tank, located at the bottom of the fuselage aft of station 258, carried 22.5 gallons of fluid, while the tank for the J33 carried only 15 gallons. The J33 was about 200 pounds heavier than the J42. Water injection was typically used on takeoff.

The XF9F-2s were equipped with the J42-P-4 engine, which ran on 100/130-octane aviation fuel mixed with 3 percent lubricating oil. This proved to be a considerable problem for the deployed aircraft carriers, particularly the older *Essex*-class, which were not configured to carry jet fuel, and fuel specialists had to mix aviation fuel with lubricating oil by hand on each occasion the Panthers were refueled. Indeed, because there were no pre-mixing facilities aboard ship to achieve the 115/145-octane gasoline (for production J42-P-4s) and 3 percent 1100 oil ratio, it was often necessary to add a quantity of gasoline, and then one gallon of oil (alternately), which slowed refueling considerably. Early F9F-2 production models were fitted with the J42-P-6 engines, which dispensed with the oil additive. Beginning with aircraft 123471, the P-8 version was installed in the F9F-2 and retrofitted in some earlier production aircraft. It featured a modified ignition system. All models offered 5,000 lbf at 12,300 rpm. The F9F-3 utilized the 4,600-lbf Allison J33-A-8, which proved to be underpowered and many, if not most, of the F9F-3s were re-engined with

*An early production F9F-3 is seen here without wingtip tanks. The tanks were added commencing with the 13th production Panther.* (Northrop Grumman History Center)

the J42-P-6, essentially making them virtually identical to the F9F-2. The J42 proved to be very reliable and was considered a fairly low-maintenance engine.

The January/February 1951 Action Report from USS *Philippine Sea* noted that its maintenance crews were pleased with the J42's performance, despite the added difficulties brought on from operating in adverse weather conditions. "The P&W J42 jet engines have operated very satisfactorily with only a minor percentage of complete engine failures. Most of the J42 engines completed their maximum 300-hour operating time limit."[xliv] However, the aircraft did have a tendency to experience flameouts during high-altitude flight in cold weather operations, "with no one determining factor as the apparent cause," although it was believed that "the altitude density compensator on the TJC-1 Main Fuel Control was one of the contributing factors, due to icing of the protective screen and frosting of the bellots [sic]."[xlv]

Pilots who flew the early Panthers were pleased with their handling qualities, but were overall critical of the underpowered engines. Walter Spangenberg, who flew several variants of the F9F during his tenure with the Navy, commented:

"The F9F-2 was an easy airplane to fly from a stick-and-throttle point of view, but it was somewhat under-powered, even with the J42 engine. The Pratt & Whitney-built Rolls-Royce Nene produced only 4,200 pounds installed thrust and required 12 seconds to spool up from idle RPM to full power. The Panther was designed with a clean wing, but because more fuel capacity was needed, it received fixed wingtip tanks and then stores on the wings, with the F9F-2B. Grumman corrected this problem with the F9F-5, which had the more powerful J48, and was widely liked by all who flew them, especially for air gunnery."[xlvi]

Spangenberg added that while the F9F-2 was bad enough, the F9F-3, with its J33, was even more

*An early production F9F-2 sits on the Grumman ramp displaying modified "scoop" ram air intakes on the fuselage spine. These were experimental and supplied less-than-optimum amounts of air to the engine. They were replaced by the large square "blow-in door" intakes, which opened inward automatically and also became a trademark feature of the F9F aircraft series.* (Naval Aviation Museum)

*An F9F-2 flies over what appears to be San Diego. The aircraft is from either VF-111 or VF-112.* (Naval Aviation Museum)

underpowered. "The J33," Spangenberg said, "was a successful engine in the F-80, the T-33, and later the T-1A, but it just did not have enough thrust for the Grumman fighters."[xlvii]

Electrical power was provided by a 24-volt, direct current, open wire system that used the aircraft structure for a ground. A generator and storage battery, together with a voltage regulator and reverse current relay, made up the overall system. Aircraft 122560 through 122589 and 123016 through 123086 were equipped with the Westinghouse DC generators, while aircraft 123397 and subsequent builds were equipped with Eclipse Type NEMA 5 combination AC/DC generators. Two external power receptacles were located on the underside of the fuselage to the left of centerline near the wing center section trailing edge; one was for engine starting only, and the second powered the entire DC system. A third receptacle for external AC power was added in the nose-wheel well beginning with aircraft 123397.

The Panther featured a simple hydraulic system, which operated the landing gear, leading- and trailing-edge flaps, speed brakes, and wing folding mechanism, and also the canopy and ejection seat. Fluid (Hydrolube Spec 51-F-22) from the reservoir in the plenum chamber is pumped by a variable-volume engine-driven pump. Two manifolds distribute pressure, a "service" manifold, which governs the wing flap controls, leading edge flaps, canopy, and brake pedals, and a "combat" manifold, which governs the armaments, dive brakes, and arresting hook. A selector value is provided to shut out pressure to all systems not essential to flight, for combat operations.

## Fuel System

The Panther possessed two large internal self-sealing fuel tanks, designated front and rear, and also carried an additional 120 gallons (720 pounds) in each wingtip tank. Described as "soft-cell" bladders, the front tank carried 442 gallons (2,658 pounds) of fuel and the rear tank contained 240 (1,440 pounds) of fuel, for a total system load of 923 gallons (5,538 pounds). The fuel system is a constant-feed system where fuel flows from the wingtip tanks to the front tank and from the rear tank to the front tank. The wingtip tanks emptied first when tip tank transfer was selected, and the fuel level in the two main tanks remained constant until the fuel level in the front tank reached 100 gallons, at which time the rear tank was emptied. A 7-gallon reserve remained enclosed in a pendulum at the bottom of the front tank, which permitted 10 seconds of inverted flight. A red jewel warning light glowed advising the pilot when he had only 1,000 pounds of fuel remaining. Refueling of the main tanks was accomplished via two refueling points on the main fuselage. A refueling point was also located on each wingtip tank.

One of the problems encountered with the Panthers during their early deployments concerned their fuel systems and the difficulties in dealing with jet fuel on the carrier. The latter problem, as noted before, not a result in any deficiency of the F9F, stemmed from the fact that *Essex*-class carriers did not carry jet fuel; rather, lubricating oil had to be added to the Panther's rear main fuel tank while the two tanks were being filled with aviation gas. Maintenance reports stated:

*The Pratt & Whitney J42 engine can be seen here, as this Panther is towed into a Navy hangar with its aft section removed. The fuselage separates at section line 299, and can be seen here being hand-pushed by a single maintenance crewman in front of the aircraft.* (National Archives via Jim Sullivan Collection)

Carrier deckhands work to refuel a Panther in Korea. The Panther lacked a single-point refueling system, thus, the wingtip tanks were refueled individually. Crewmembers used a specially designed ladder to access the tank with the wings folded for deck storage. Flight with fuel in the wingtip tanks was limited to Mach .80 at all altitudes due to buffeting exhibited when the tanks weren't empty. (Jim Sullivan Collection)

A Panther conducts a fuel dump from the wingtip tanks. Rumor has it that some pilots from the U.S. Navy Blue Angels aerobatic team witnessed a Grumman demonstration of this capability and used it as the basis for their colored smoke release during performances. (Northrop Grumman History Center)

"The present arrangement for use of oil proportioners [sic] for mixing jet fuel is not satisfactory for flight deck use in cold weather. The oil will not flow properly during cold weather and it is necessary to use regular gasoline cans to pour warm oil in the main tanks of jet aircraft."[xlviii]

The former, however, was the result of the Panther's fuel system configuration, which required the wingtip tanks to be fueled directly at the tank. As reported in the USS *Antietam*'s (CV-36) Action Report:

"The main problem encountered in servicing aircraft with fuel has been refueling of jet aircraft with their wings folded. This necessitates the use of wing ladders and experiments to date have not resulted in a satisfactory ladder. The ladder must be light in weight yet strong enough to withstand constant heavy usage. New ladders of thin-walled steel tubing are on order and it is hoped they will provide the answer."[xlix]

The refueling of wingtip tanks was quite dangerous for flight deck crews, as many had to mount the ladders and work more than 20 feet above a pitching flight deck, often at times when the aircraft was positioned close to the flight deck edge.

## Communications and Navigation

The Panther carried a rather sophisticated communications and navigation suite for a fighter aircraft. On early F9F-2 and -3 models (BuNos 122560 through 122571), the communications consisted of the AN/ARC-1 VHF radio, which offered 10-channel (one of which was Guard), two-way voice line-of-sight communications. Navigation was handled by the AN/ARR-2A radio homing receiver, and the AN/ARC-5 radio ranger receiver. The ARR-1 operated on a line-of-sight range while the ARC-5 had an effective range of 150 miles. An

Communication controls on the Panther were located on the right-hand cockpit console. The numbered knob in the center is the channel selector for the ARC-1 UHF radio. Vertical rows of circuit breakers can be seen on the console's inner wall at left of photo. (Northrop Grumman History Center)

AN/APX-1 IFF device provided aircraft identification and the AN/APN-1, added on aircraft 122560 through 123713, served as a radio altimeter. The APN-1 was designed to provide direct measurement of altitude relative to the terrain during flight within a low range of 0 to 400 feet and a high range of 400 to 4,000 feet. When operating in the high range, the altitude limit switch settings were actually 10 times the numbers shown on the dial.

Beginning with aircraft 122572, the ARC-1 was supplemented with the ARC-27, which had 1,750 channels, from which any 18 or 20 channels might be available to the pilot, as well as UHF capability. The ARC-27 provided AM radio communications between the airplane and any other station similarly equipped within the ultra high frequency range of 225.0 to 399.9 megacycles. The APN-6 also replaced the APN-1 radio altimeter. The AN/ARN-6 radio compass, with a range of 100 miles, was also added as was the AN/APG-30 gun ranging radar (BuNo 123397 onward). The APX-6 replaced the APX-1. The majority of the communications gear was located in the aircraft's nose section. As the illustration shows, the communications and navigation gear continued to grow over the Panther's life.

## Landing Gear

The F9F Panther featured a tricycle landing gear configured such that the main gear retracted into the

*The Panther's nose wheel is shown here.* (Jose Ramos)

fuselage and the nose gear retracted aft. The main gear tires were 14-ply and measured 24 by 5.5 inches and were inflated to 160 psi for land operations and 200 psi for carrier operations. The nose gear tire was 10-ply and measured 16 by 5.80, inflated to 175 psi for both land- and carrier-based operations. Brakes consisted of a single disc per wheel and were controlled by the rudder pedals once speeds fell below 70 knots. Carrier operations during the early months of the Korean War indicated that the nose wheel was not strong enough for repeated carrier landings and a strengthened nose gear was added.

## Catapult Bridle and Tailhook

As it was primarily designed for operations from the deck of an aircraft carrier, the Panther possessed both a bridle launch system for catapult launching and a tailhook for use with arresting gear. Panthers were launched using a towing pendant attached just aft of the nose gear. The aircraft was then simultaneously restrained by the hold-back fitting, located aft of the main landing gear. When stressed, the hold-back would break loose and the aircraft would be catapulted down the carrier deck. Launch speeds ranged from 114 to 120 knots, depending on the Panther's load and the wind-over-deck. Wind-over-deck also impacted the external ordnance that could be carried by the Panther.

Carrier landings were accomplished using the aircraft's tailhook, which was attached below the tailpipe. Panthers featured a sting tailhook that was manually retracted into the rear fuselage beneath the jet exhaust by deck crew after the carrier landing. The maximum permitted arresting hook load was 60,000 pounds, and the maximum deceleration was 4.22 gs. A tail skid was also provided to protect the tailpipe during landings. Initially, manually operated provisions were added in aircraft 122563, 122572, and subsequent examples for a hydraulic system, which was interconnected with the arresting hook so that it automatically lowered with the tailhook. On a portion of the production models (BuNos 122560

*The main landing gear can be seen in this F9F-5 photograph.* (Jose Ramos)

The Panther's tail hook and exhaust can be seen in this photograph looking forward. (Jose Ramos)

through 122571), the guns were automatically set to safety when the hook was lowered; this was further modified to safety the guns when the landing gear was moved to "down" beginning with aircraft 122572. A typical carrier approach in an F9F-2 or -3 was about 114 knots.

Concerning the Panther's handling around the carrier, Walter Spangenberg made the following observations:

"Carrier qualification in the underpowered, slow-to-accelerate F9F-2 on the straight deck carrier *Philippine Sea*, which usually had aircraft parked forward, was both frustrating and dangerous. The F9F-2's approach speed was around 115 to 120 knots, depending on fuel aboard and we did not have the angle-of-attack indicators, which were fitted some years later. The jet engine decelerated more slowly than a reciprocating engine at the cut, so the LSO had to commit to either a cut or a wave-off when the aircraft was much further away on its approach. It was more difficult for everyone involved to get it right, but eventually most of us did, most of the time.

We flew a World War II–style carrier landing pattern, widened to accommodate the Panther's higher speed and wider turning radius. We also flew the carrier approach and indeed all landing approaches, with our belly-mounted speed brakes extended, to increase drag and thereby increase the power setting required. This gave us better engine response, shortening the time to accelerate to full power for a possible wave-off, but it also increased fuel consumption and thereby decreased the number of passes one could make between maximum landing weight and bingo fuel weight."[l]

Despite the early Panther's powerplant problems, it was nevertheless regarded as an outstanding jet fighter.

At least one of the aircraft carrier Action Reports generated during the Korean War addressed the Panther's handling characteristics around the boat. In its Action Report for the period 1 January to 1 February 1951, the USS *Philippine Sea* (CV-47) concluded, "it is generally felt that carrier landings in the F9F-2 type aircraft are accomplished with far greater ease than in conventional types."[li] Moreover, the Action Report continued "no major problems have been encountered in [the Panther] squadrons during the Korean Campaign." Nevertheless, it made the following observations and recommendations concerning F9F-2 operations:

A Panther prepares to launch. The F9F-2 used a bridle that attached to the catapult system and helped propel the aircraft down the flight deck. The expendable bridle was then cast off the front of the carrier's flight deck after separating from the airborne aircraft. (Northrop Grumman History Center)

"It is highly desirable to have approximately 200 yards, "in the groove" to take care of any minor corrections with regard to "lining up" and adjusting speed. The landing signal officer does not have as good a speed indication on the landing jet aircraft as he is able to have on the conventional types and it is necessary for the pilot to adjust his speed within safe limits before he takes his attention from the cockpit instruments completely and focuses his attention on the landing signal officer. With the excellent visibility that is afforded the pilot in the F9F, he is able to make these minor correc-

tions in speed and alignment in the groove and at the same time be under the control of the landing signal officer. There has been a tendency on the part of some pilots to leave too much of a speed correction for the straightaway and this has resulted in reduction of too much throttle to lose excess speed with consequent settling at the ramp."[lii]

The Action Report further noted:

"The proper handling of the aircraft after the cut still remains the most important part of the recovery. Pilot error involving diving for the deck is still noted and must

*This photograph provides an excellent view of the Panther's aerodynamically clean underside and intake ducts. Note the "Swiss cheese" perforations in the speed brakes seen just forward of the air intakes. This was done to reduce air loads and buffeting when the brakes were opened.* (Northrop Grumman History Center)

*Underside view (looking forward) of this F9F-2 reveals light damage sustained in an emergency landing. The left main tire has shredded the grass and debris can be seen elsewhere, possibly the result of brake failure and subsequent runway overrun. Underside fuselage flaps aft of the main wheel well are visible in the deployed position. These flaps were used in conjunction with the speed brakes to both reduce and control the Panther's speed and rate of descent.* (Northrop Grumman History Center)

*In cases where a Panther lost or broke its hook, the aircraft was recovered using a double-tiered barrier system seen here catching this Navy Panther. In such cases, touch-down speeds were held as low as possible.* (Northrop Grumman History Center)

*The Panther adapted well to the carrier environment. Here, a Marine F9F-2 lowers its wings and maneuvers on the flight deck prior to launch.* (Northrop Grumman History Center)

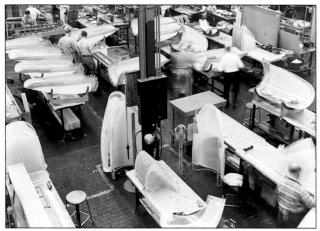

Workers at Grumman assemble Plexiglas canopy sections for the Panther, seen here still wearing their protective adhesive paper coatings. (Northrop Grumman History Center)

The ARA-25 directional antenna is contained in the bulged fairing under the nose section of this Panther shown wearing the later-1950s Navy gull-gray-with-white color scheme. (Naval Aviation Museum)

Straining to catch an arresting cable, this Panther settles awkwardly onto the carrier deck in a very nose-high attitude. Carrier landings were typically made at 108 to 110 knots, with 1,000 pounds of fuel left in the tanks. One knot was added to the approach speed for each 200 pounds of fuel over this 1,000-pound mark. The Panther's engines were operated at 65 percent RPM during approach so that full thrust could be quickly applied in the event of a waive-off. (Northrop Grumman History Center)

be attributed to the high landing speed and excellent visibility, which combine to render the impression of a too-rapid advance along the deck. Both squadrons have adopted the policy of landing aboard with the flaps in the "TAKE-OFF" position. There has been no damage to the inboard flap sections and "TAKE-OFF" flaps have provided a cushioning effect on landing which has proved to be highly desirable."[liii]

Recommendations were also made to modify the break-up and rendezvous procedures to make the flights more manageable for air traffic controllers.

Similar suggestions were found regarding carrier catapult launch operations. The same Action Report observed:

"Catapulting of F9F-2 type aircraft in low relative wind conditions and high gross weights imposed several problems during the early months of the Korean Campaign. It is felt that the warm climatic conditions that prevailed at that time, plus the lower static thrust of the P-6 engine, created a marginal safety feature during launch. It is imperative that full power be maintained throughout the launch. This has imposed no problem in the later model aircraft (which have the throttle friction control lock), but in the earlier models, inadvertent retarding of the throttle was experienced in many cases. The pilot's hand should remain free of the throttle during initial acceleration and then be put on the throttle to ensure that full power is being utilized. He should grip the stick firmly with his right hand and thereby fly the aircraft off the deck under positive control. A tab setting of one and three-quarters to two degrees "BACK" has been found to be very satisfactory."[liv]

The carrier also developed its own wind/weight table for use during F9F-2 launches from the H-4B catapult, which minimized abnormal accelerations. For a relative wind over deck of 30 knots, the catapult accumulator dome pressure was set at 3,500 psi. For each 2-knot increase in wind over deck, the pressure was reduced by 100 psi. This not only adequately addressed the problem but the problem completely disappeared when Panthers featured the P-8 engine.

### Flight Operations

While the Panther was described as a highly maneuverable aircraft, it nonetheless had some limitations of its flight envelope. According to the Flight Manual[lv], the following maneuvers were permitted with or without external stores:

- Aileron Roll
- Inverted Flight (not to exceed 10 seconds)
- Vertical Turn
- Wingover
- Chandelle
- Loop
- Immelmann Turn

Intentional spins and snap rolls were prohibited, and stalls were not to be continued beyond the start of buffeting. Maneuvering with trim tabs was also prohibited. Abrupt rudder maneuvers were permitted to 300 pounds pedal force up to 430 knots, but abrupt rudder reversals were prohibited. The following air speed limitations also applied to flight operations:

- Landing flaps, 165 knots
- Landing gear, 215 knots
- Canopy open, 215 knots
- Dive brakes, no limitations

Landing with fuel in the wingtip tanks was prohibited.

Although the Panther's spin and recovery characteristics were deemed good, flight tests demonstrated a large loss in altitude accompanying the spin. "Flight tests have shown that although recovery can be effected [sic] in less than one turn, from 4,000 to 7,000 feet may be needed for recovery."[lvi] Pilots could usually recover in less than one turn after initiation of normal recovery procedures. Recovery could also be obtained by merely relaxing the flight controls. The aircraft's elevator was the primary control for spin recovery.

### The F9F-2P

A photoreconnaissance version of the F9F-2 flew during the Korean War as a result of the Navy's realization, when the war began in June 1950, that it was without a jet-powered reconnaissance aircraft. At the time, orders had been placed for a reconnaissance version of the F2H-2, but those were still months away and the carrier air groups needed something immediately. As a result of the demand, the Navy modified a small fraction of the F9F-2s to serve as unarmed photoreconnaissance aircraft. To accomplish this conversion, the four 20mm cannons as well as the AN/APG-30 radar-ranging system were removed from the nose section and an oblique and vertical camera were added, together with a small window cut into the bottom of each side from which the cameras could be aimed. The left, right, and main consoles were rearranged to remove controls used for the armament system and replaced with controls for the additional photographic equipment.

The cameras were contained in two bays (forward and rear); the forward bay housed the fixed-mount vertical camera—either the Fairchild K-17 12-inch, K-17 6-inch, or CA-8 cameras, or the S-7-S Sonne continuous strip camera—while the rear bay housed one of the following rotary mounted cameras—the 3-, 15-, or 30-degree K-18 24-inch camera or 3-, 15-, or 30-degree K-17 24-inch camera or three fixed Trimetrogon K-17 6-inch cameras. Approximately 100 pounds of ballast was also installed as fixed equipment between stations 12 and 25, to ensure the aircraft maintained the proper center of gravity, with an optional 120 pounds of additional

An F9F-2P from VMJ-3 is shown with its nose section slid forward. The guns were removed on photo Panthers and the nose section was reconfigured to accommodate two camera bays. The cameras took photos through glass viewing windows, such as the port window seen here directly above the aircraft's nose strut. (Jim Sullivan Collection)

A detail view of the F9F-2P's camera bay looking downward shows two of the oblique-angle cameras. This variant of the Panther was the first jet-powered photoreconnaissance aircraft ever used in Navy service. (Jim Sullivan Collection)

An F9F-2P photo reconnaissance Panther from VC-61 Det D is parked on the aft carrier deck. (Robert Tallman)

ballast when the lighter cameras were used. Access to the camera bays was obtained through a hatch on the top of the nose. The A-10VF photographic viewfinder was added in the forward part of the cockpit.

## F9F-2P Camera Equipment

The following equipment is optional for
photo reconnaissance missions

| Location | Equipment | Type Mount | Optical Axis |
|---|---|---|---|
| Forward Camera Bay | S-7-S Sonne Continuous Strip Camera | Fixed | Vertical |
| | or | | |
| | K-17 12-inch | Fixed | Vertical |
| | or | | |
| | K-17 6-inch | Fixed | Vertical |
| | or | | |
| | CA-8 | Fixed | Vertical |
| Rear Camera Bay | K-18 24-inch with A-7 or A-8 Magazine | Rotary | 3°, 15°, and 90° below horizontal |
| | or | | |
| | K-17 24-inch with A-5 or A-9 Magazine | Rotary | 3°, 15°, and 90° below horizontal |
| | or | | |
| | Three K-17 6-inch | Rotary | Trimetrogon |

The K-18 aircraft camera was used for making high-altitude, large-scale, vertical, and spotting photographs, while the K-17 camera was designed to take vertical and spotting photographs. Equipped with a 6-inch f:6.3 metrogen lens, the CA-8 camera was used for precision mapping and was an automatic camera designed for making a series of aerial photographs for mapping and charting. The accompanying MA-6 magazine held approximately 250 nine-by-nine inch negatives on a 200-ft film roll. The S-7-S Sonne continuous strip camera was used specifically for taking sharp vertical photographs at low altitude and high speeds.

A photo recorder was located on the forward nose bay, which included the following equipment: radio altimeter repeater indicator, sensitive altimeter, airspeed indicator, flasher and relay unit, remove compass repeater indicator, clock, outside temperature indicator, film speed indicator, three digit subtractor-type counter, and a AN-N-6A camera.

Designated as F9F-2P, most of these reconnaissance aircraft deployed with two- or three-plane detachments from Composite Squadron VC-61 and were assigned the tail code markings "PP," referred to as "Papa Papa." Because the F9F-2Ps were unarmed, they were always escorted by at least one other Panther. Photoreconnaissance missions would typically begin at 10,000 feet and the photo runs could take the aircraft down to just a few hundred feet off the ground. As Walter

*A row of Panthers is seen here on the ATU-206 flight line.* (Bert Kinzey, Detail & Scale, Inc.)

*Sporting "barber pole" striping on its wingtip tanks, an F9F-2 from ATU-206 at NAS Pensacola takes off for a training mission. Panthers quickly found their way into the training command once they were replaced by the swept-wing Cougar.* (Northrop Grumman History Center)

*This VF-21 F9F-3 Panther is seen still rolling after missing all the arresting cables while attempting to land on the USS Midway (VCB-41) in November 1951. The jet will shortly tear through the restraining barrier and crash into other aircraft spotted on the carrier's foredeck. Such was naval aircraft carrier operations before the advent of angled flight decks that safely allowed waive-offs and go-arounds.* (Jim Sullivan Collection)

A Marine Panther's front landing gear collapses as it skips over the barricade. (Jim Sullivan Collection)

A VF-92 Panther prepares to grab a wire aboard USS Philippine Sea (CV-47). Note the abundance of wires available to catch the aircraft. With modern approach lighting and guidance systems today, a modern carrier has only four widely spaced arresting cables, with the fabled "three wire" as the prize catch for a pilot. (Jim Sullivan Collection)

The small opening seen here under the "144" insignia is the air intake for the avionics and gun bay ventilation systems. (Northrop Grumman History Center)

Spangenberg said in his interview, "the crews flying the photo planes at the 1,500 feet altitude and 250 knots required to get good pictures with the original photo equipment quickly realized that such flights made them a sitting duck for any gunner in the area."[lvii] A fleet modification consisting of an "image motion compensator," which rotated the camera from forward to aft while the shutter was open, enabled crews to fly both lower and faster, and thereby improved survivability. The F9F-2Ps operated regularly off U.S. carriers until deployment of the F9F-5P Panthers starting in late 1951. F9F-2Ps also flew with VMJ-1, Hedron-33, VF-721, VU-1, and VMF-311.

## Other F9F-2 Designations

Three other F9F-2 designations existed, two of which were not true combat aircraft, but rather drones, and one, the F9F-2B, will be discussed later in Chapter Four. A few F9F-2s were designated as F9F-2Ds and modified as unarmed radio-controlled drones. Remote control equipment was substituted in the nose section in place of the 20mm cannons. Other aircraft controlled the F9F-2Ds, including the F9F-2KD, which was modified as a drone director. The drones were flown largely by Navy Utility (VU) squadrons, Guided Missile Groups (GMGU-1 and -2), and at the Naval Ordnance Test Station (NOTS) at China Lake and NAS Point Mugu in California well into the 1960s. The aircraft serving as drones were fitted with autopilot and remote control features that permitted total control of their flight regime. Having maneuverable drones meant that new weapons systems could be tested in more realistic scenarios rather than simply intercepting targets flying a straight and level course.

## F9F-2 and F9F-3 Operational History

Following the conclusion of the Navy's Board of Inspection (BIS) Trials and carrier suitability tests in early 1949, both versions of the Panther were declared fit for service and began entering the fleet. The same production delays that had hampered flight testing also lead to the delays of the first flight of the initial production aircraft. Because of delays with the J42, the F9F-3 was the first production Panther to attain flight, accomplishing this in January 1949. The first production F9F-2 flew in August 1949.

## F9F-2 Production

A total of 566 F9F-2 Panthers were built, including two XF9F-2s (BuNos 122475 and 122477) and 564 F9F-2s (BuNos 122563, 122567, 122569-122570, 122572, 122586-122589, 123016-123019, 123044-123067, 123077-123083, 123397-123713, 125083-125155, and 127086-127215). Three planned F9F-2s, aircraft numbers 123084, 123085, and 123086, were built as the XF9F-4, XF9F-5, and XF9F-4/-5 static airframe.

*Flight testing for the Panther was largely handled by NATC. Shown here is an F9F-2.* (Steve Ginter)

### F9F-3 Production

Fifty-five F9F-3s were built, including the lone prototype (BuNo 122476) and 54 F9F-3s (BuNos 122560-122562, 122564-122566, 122568, 122571, 122573-122585, 123020-123043, and 123068-123076).

Because of the delays noted, the F9F-3 was actually the first production Panther delivered to the fleet. On 8 May 1949, VF-51, then stationed at NAS San Diego, received its first Panthers. The F9F-2 was assigned to the

*An F9F-2 Panther is removed from the arresting gear while another is waived off. Visible as a speck in the background is a third Panther beginning its roll into the groove as it prepares for final approach.* (Bert Kinzey)

Blue Angels in late August 1949, and then a few weeks later to VMF-115, the first USMC squadron to receive the Panther. The Navy's first fleet squadron to operate the F9F-2 was VF-111, also stationed at NAS San Diego. VF-31 was the first East Coast squadron to operate the Panther, having received its first F9F-2 in December 1949, along with four experienced pilots from VF-51 to assist with transition. Fieldwork was completed in the early spring and carrier qualifications were completed on 6 April aboard USS *Philippine Sea* (CV-47) after 286 landings.

By mid-1950, the Navy had eight squadrons equipped with Panthers, including two F9F-3 squadrons, VF-51 and VF-52, aboard USS *Valley Forge* (CV-45), which was the first U.S. Navy carrier to launch air strikes against North Korea during the Korean War. (A more detailed discussion of the Panther's involvement in the Korean War is found in Chapter Six.) During the early 1950s, the F9F-2 and F9F-3 served in 22 U.S. Navy active squadrons, at least 15 Reserve squadrons, and six Marine Corps squadrons, providing the bulwark of the Navy and Marine Corps' air-to-ground attack capability. Although the Panther distinguished itself in Korea, the introduction of the high-performance swept-wing jets during the mid-1950s meant that the Panther's career would be a short but notable one. By 1956, the F9F-2 and F9F-3 Panthers had been phased out of operational fleet squadrons and saw service primarily with Navy Reserve units, Auxiliary Training Units (ATUs), and in the training command. The last Marine Corps units, VMF-213 and VMF-234 based in Minneapolis, were retired in 1958.

A colorful view of an F9F-2B at sea parked on a carrier deck during the Korean War. When the war began, Navy Panthers were used in the air superiority fighter role and also performed strafing runs using their 20mm cannons. True air-to-ground capability was added with the F9F-2B, which deployed with VMA-311 and Navy fleet squadrons beginning in January 1951. Note the propeller-driven Douglas AD Skyraiders and Vought F4U Corsairs parked with their wings folded in the background. (Northrop Grumman Center)

A Marine Corps Panther is seen in front of the island of the carrier Franklin D. Roosevelt (CVB-42). (Steve Ginter)

Photo Panther pilots enjoyed panting nicknames on their Panthers, like this "Peepin' Tom" painted on a VC-61 F9F-2P. Other more famous names were "Like," "Look," and "Pic." Notice the pilot's colorful name, Lt. Papa San Young. (Steve Ginter)

A VF-51 F9F-2 and VC-61 F9F-2P are readied for missions. The crew appears to be working on the Panther's guns. (Steve Ginter)

# A Pilot Speaks:
# Conversation with Walter
# Spangenberg on Flying the Panther

"Returning from Korea with Air Group 102 in *Bon Homme Richard* in December 1951, I was detached and ordered to the pre-commissioning group for Air Group NINE in Alameda, California. Air Group NINE was to have VF-91 and VF-93 flying the F9F-2 Panther, VF-92 and VF-94 flying the F4U-4 Corsair, and VA-95 flying the AD-2/3/4 aircraft. I was assigned to VF-91, joining a growing group of officers coming from various places, none from currently active squadrons. We were all excited about transitioning to jets, but there were no jets available for us yet. We were assigned one, two, then three FG-1 D Corsairs to use for proficiency maintenance until Panthers could be provided. We proudly painted the Corsairs in VF-91 colors, and found they were fun to fly; actually a little lighter and faster than the F4U-4 at low and medium altitudes.

"Air Group NINE was re-commissioned on 25 March 1952. And finally, two worn and tired, ready for overhaul F9F-2 aircraft arrived for VF-91 and two more for VF-93. We gave up the FG-1 Ds and got to work on being a jet squadron. We had one officer in the squadron—indeed the only officer in either VF-91 or VF-93—who had flown jets. Lt. Fred Turnbull had flown FJ-1 Furies in the Reserves at NAS Oakland, and with his help, along with the Pilot's Handbook and the local Grumman Rep, we taught ourselves to fly the F9F-2 Panther. There were no replacement training squadrons in those days; only the Jet Transition Training Unit at Pensacola, which was not available to pilots already in the Fleet and too small anyway to accommodate the numbers that would have been required.

"The F9F-2 was an easy airplane to fly from a stick-and-throttle point of view, but was somewhat underpowered with the J42 engine (a Pratt & Whitney-built Rolls-Royce Nene) developing only 4,200 lbf installed, and requiring 12 seconds to spool up from idle RPM to full power. The Panther had been designed by Grumman with a clean wing; then because more fuel capacity was needed, it got fixed wingtip tanks and then store stations on the wings. Grumman and the Navy soon corrected this situation by putting the more powerful J48 engine in the F9F-5, which was widely liked by all who flew them, especially for aerial gunnery.

"The F9F-2 was bad enough, but the Navy caved-in to an uproar in Congress instigated by Drew Pearson, an editorial columnist for the *Washington Post*, who raised a huge to-do about the Navy buying engines for the Panther only from Pratt & Whitney when an alternate engine was available in the J33, built by the Allison Division of General Motors. The Navy then bought the J33, which had only 3,600 lbf (!) for the F9F-3, and subsequently repeated that for the F9F-7 Cougar with a later version of the J33. These airplanes were so underpowered that neither was ever deployed for use aboard ship, and both were ultimately converted to F9F-2 and F9F-6 configurations. Actually, the J33 was a successful engine in the F-80, the T-33, and later, the T-1A; it just did not have enough thrust for the Grumman fighters.

"There were many amusing incidents in our self-taught training cycle. We had, of course, a general syllabus of qualifications needed for each pilot to be ready for deployment aboard ship, but our training cycle was shorter than the normal peacetime 18 months, with Air Group NINE scheduled to deploy in *Philippine Sea* in December of 1952, and we did not have a full complement of F9F-2 aircraft until July, as I recall. Our squadron Operations Department had to prioritize and concentrate our training flights on the most vital portions of the desired syllabus. In the middle of all this, somehow Air Group NINE was chosen to be the test case for the use of Hydrolube, a new non-flammable hydraulic fluid, which promised to eliminate the danger of hydraulic fires as a result of combat damage.

"The stuff was yellow colored, and apparently less viscous than the familiar red fluid then in general use, and we had many more than the expected number of hydraulic leaks. One VA-95 aircraft came back from a training flight one day with the blue paint gone from the whole aft port side of the fuselage as a result of a hydraulic leak, and we had a real surprise one Monday morning to come to work and find one of our aircraft in the hangar leaning over to the right at a very unusual angle. It turned out that the Panther had no mechanical down-lock safety pin to be installed in the landing gear after flight, but had what was described by the Grumman people as an internal hydraulic lock. Well, the internal hydraulic lock had gotten tired in the presence of Hydrolube apparently, and the right main landing gear had partially folded! The entire Air Group was back to using the old familiar red fluid before deployment.

"We had first to learn to fly a jet airplane, and it early became apparent that we had to pay a lot more attention to fuel management than we had done in props, where one could go out on a training flight of any sort and expect to come back with fuel to spare. Not so in the Panther. Those fixed tip tanks would hold about 125 gallons each, and there was no fuel gauge for those tanks. Fuel was transferred under dynamic air pressure from an orifice in the nose of each tank when the pilot selected tip tank transfer with a switch in the cockpit. Normal procedure when based ashore was to turn on the switch early in the flight, transfer all of the tip tank fuel, and turn off the switch before landing. Since the tanks could not be dropped, there was also a tip tank dump valve in the pointed tail end of the each tank which was also controlled by a switch in the cockpit. On a short flight, the extra tip tank fuel was normally dumped at altitude before landing. This proved to be a booby trap when a pilot dumped fuel and failed to close the dump valves—a large fuel spill resulted on the ramp when the aircraft was refueled if the plane captain failed to check the cockpit switch before refueling. Our plane captains soon got wise to this, but more than once on a cross-country flight to a station not familiar with the Panther there was much uproar and gnashing of teeth by the local Ops Duty Officer.

"In our abbreviated training cycle, we did deploy the squadron to what was then an Auxiliary Landing Field at Fallon, Nevada, for weapons training. Our training with bombs, rockets, and aerial gunnery was abbreviated even more when we found that in the underpowered F9F-2 we had to launch with only 50 gallons of fuel in each tip tank in order to get off safely at 4,000 feet above sea level and daytime temperatures of 100 degrees or so Fahrenheit. The longest runway at Fallon was then about 7,000 feet long, and we still often went through a dust cloud at the end from the preceding aircraft. We also found that the electric elevator trim in our 125-series airplanes was less satisfactory than the manual cable in the 123-series because it worked too slowly to keep up with increasing aircraft speed in a dive. Our training scheme ran parallel with that of VF-93: We had made no arrangement with them to designate one squadron as air-to-air and one as air-to-ground. It would never have worked anyway, once we were deployed, since the squadrons were quite competitive and neither would want to see the other designated for a perceived advantage of any sort.

"One maneuver we practiced in our training was new with the transition to jets, and actually sort of a fun game: the simulated flameout approach. Following the key points and altitudes diagrammed in the Pilot's Handbook, we would hit the high key over the intended landing point with gear, flaps, and speed brakes extended and engine power set at idle; then make a left 360-degree circling approach to a touch-and-go landing. It quickly became a point of pride with each pilot to be able to do this with precision, and it was good practice against the time when a pilot might have an engine failure at high altitude. We did just enough cross-country, simulated instrument and night flying to comply with minimums required in our training syllabus. There was no time available for more.

"At the end of the summer it became time to get busy with field carrier landing practice and preparations for going aboard ship for pilot carrier qualification. Fortunately, we were a day fighter squadron and there was no requirement to qualify at night. We had a landing signal officer in the air group who had not worked with jets before, and that did not help matters. We never did Field Carrier Landing Practice (FCLP) at NAS Alameda, because it would interfere too much with normal NAS air traffic, but would fly over the hills to the Auxiliary Landing Field (ALF) at Crow's Landing with a reduced fuel load, make about six passes at the deck lined out on the runway there, land, refuel, and debrief with the LSO while another group of planes was practicing, then get in our planes to make another six passes or so, and fly back to Alameda. The fuel load for this practice was calculated to be close to the fuel load that we would have in work at sea with the carrier. This was a critical item because too much fuel aboard would put the plane over the max landing weight, and too little fuel would put the plane below the bingo fuel needed to fly to the nearest available runway in case of a foul deck problem aboard ship. The difference was enough fuel for about six passes at Crow's Landing, but often for only three aboard ship, depending on how far the ship was from an available landing field. Carrier qualification was usually done in Southern California waters with a San Diego-based carrier, but there was in those days no auxiliary landing strip on San Clemente Island, so the nearest field would usually be either Miramar or North Island.

"Carrier qualification in the under-powered, slow-to-accelerate F9F-2 on the straight deck carrier *Philippine Sea*, which had the then-standard 12 arresting wires, the Davis barrier for jets, a palisade barrier forward to be raised when needed, and usually parked aircraft forward, was both frustrating and dangerous. The F9F-2's carrier approach speed was around 115 to 120 knots, depending on fuel aboard, and we did not have the angle-of-attack indicators, which were fitted some years later. The jet engine decelerated more slowly than a recap at the cut, so the LSO had to commit to either a cut or a wave off when the aircraft was much farther away on its approach. It was more difficult for everyone involved to get it right, but eventually most of us did, most of the time.

"We flew a 600-foot WWII-style carrier landing pattern, widened to accommodate the Panther's higher speed and wider turning radius. We also flew the carrier approach, and indeed all landing approaches, with our belly-mounted speed brakes extended, to increase drag and thereby increase the power setting required. This gave us better engine response, shortening the time to accelerate to full power for a possible wave off, but it also increased fuel consumption and thereby decreased the number of passes one could make between maximum landing weight and bingo fuel weight.

"In early December we packed everything and moved the Air Wing to San Diego to go aboard *Philippine Sea* and begin our deployment to WestPac by way of Hawaii for the prescribed Operational Readiness Inspection (ORI). The ORI went fairly well in the air, as I recall, with airborne observers flying with us on practice missions using targets on the uninhabited island of Kahoolawe. We did not do well around the ship, however, and in both Panther squadrons aroused sufficient concern on the part of the staff that it was decided to augment our Air Wing LSO with one who was more experienced in waving jets. During the course of this flail the ship was required to conduct a full power run and could not meet the expected speed. Divers were sent down and it was discovered that three of the ship's four propellers were damaged, apparently resulting from running over a ditched aircraft on a previous cruise. The shipyard at Pearl Harbor had one replacement propeller, but the other two required shipment from the continental United States (CONUS), and then the ship would have to be dry-docked to have the propellers replaced. This added up to a three-week delay in our departure for WestPac, so the Air Wing was shore based at NAS Barbers Point and the two jet squadrons used the time for a thorough workup with our new LSO. An unintended byproduct of this delay was Christmas in Honolulu, with firecrackers going off everywhere!

"Although we were still learning to get aboard the boat during our December 1952 Operational Readiness Inspection in Hawaiian waters, by the time we got into our first line period in the Sea of Japan off the east coast of Korea, most of the jet recoveries were routine. Routine, that is, until we started breaking tailhook points and "routinely" screaming down the deck over all 12 wires and into the Davis barrier. This gets a pilot's attention the first time it occurs, but damage to the airplane was usually limited to the main landing gear doors, and often the airplane was back in the air the same day. The cause of all this excitement was traced to improperly machined hook points, which had a stress-concentrating sharp inside corner at which they broke after a few landing arrestments. This diagnosis by Cdr. Sonnenschein, the ship's engineering officer, led to a quick solution and that problem went away."

*In a scene repeated countless times during the Korean War, Navy aircrews climb to a carrier's flight deck after their pre-mission briefing in the ready room below. These F9F-2 pilots are from VF-721 aboard the USS Boxer (CV 21).* (Northrop Grumman History Center)

# CHAPTER FOUR

# PANTHER ARMAMENT

*The Panther's claws came in many different forms. Here we see three High Velocity Airborne Rockets (HVAR) being carried under each wing of an F9F-2B. Although the -2B was deployed to Korea aboard carriers beginning in January 1951, it did not actually deliver bombs until 2 April when VF-191 struck a North Korean railroad bridge near Songjin. Up to that time, the Panthers used a combination of cannon fire and rockets.* (Northrop Grumman History Center)

When it was designed in the mid to late 1940s, the Panther was originally intended as a jet-powered carrier-based day fighter. However, due to a variety of reasons, namely the superior performance of the swept-wing MiG-15s encountered over North Korea, the Panther shifted its role to become the Navy's primary air-to-ground attack aircraft. Reflecting its original fighter mission, the Panther was armed with four Hispano-Suiza Mk 3 20mm cannons mounted in the aircraft's nose section. Each gun held 190 rounds of ammunition (760 rounds total), which were stored in four ammunition boxes connected to the guns by feed chutes. In early Panthers, two of the ammunition boxes were located just above the cannons, with two located under the pilot's seat; this arrangement was changed for aircraft 122560 to 122564, 122566 to 122568, and 122570 to 122571, and for these aircraft, all four boxes were located under the pilot's seat. The added room above the guns was used for more electronics. Each gun was charged by an Aero 13A hydraulic charger.

The Panther's cannon fired at the rate of 10 rounds per second. Ammunition belts typically contained three types of ammo in continuous order: HEI, or High Explosive Incendiary; AP, or Armor Piercing; and Tracer. As former Navy F9F pilot George Schnitzer explained in his book, *Panthers Over Korea*, "The HEI was very

*An F9F-2 from VF-71 aboard USS* Tarawa. *(CV 40), is seen here in spring 1951 being prepared for a training mission. The squadron later deployed to Korea aboard USS* Bon Homme Richard *(CV 31) from 20 May 1952 through 8 June 1953. Notice the ATAR rockets affixed to the wings. These proved effective against North Korean tanks.* (Naval Aviation Museum)

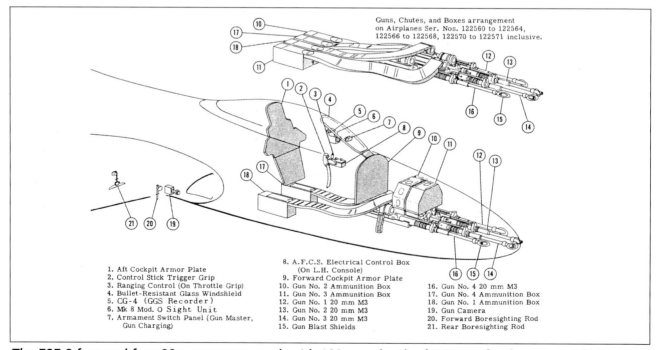

Guns, Chutes, and Boxes arrangement on Airplanes Ser. Nos. 122560 to 122564, 122566 to 122568, 122570 to 122571 inclusive.

1. Aft Cockpit Armor Plate
2. Control Stick Trigger Grip
3. Ranging Control (On Throttle Grip)
4. Bullet-Resistant Glass Windshield
5. CG-4 (GGS Recorder)
6. Mk 8 Mod. 0 Sight Unit
7. Armament Switch Panel (Gun Master, Gun Charging)
8. A.F.C.S. Electrical Control Box (On L.H. Console)
9. Forward Cockpit Armor Plate
10. Gun No. 2 Ammunition Box
11. Gun No. 3 Ammunition Box
12. Gun No. 1 20 mm M3
13. Gun No. 2 20 mm M3
14. Gun No. 3 20 mm M3
15. Gun Blast Shields
16. Gun No. 4 20 mm M3
17. Gun No. 4 Ammunition Box
18. Gun No. 1 Ammunition Box
19. Gun Camera
20. Forward Boresighting Rod
21. Rear Boresighting Rod

*The F9F-2 featured four 20mm cannons, each with 190 rounds. The four guns fired at a rate of 10 rounds per second. The F9F-2 had two ammunition storage configurations: One had two ammunition boxes located over the guns and two boxes under the pilot's seating area, and the other had all four boxes located under the pilot's seat.* (Flight Manual for the F9F-2 and F9F-3 Airplane)

The Panther's four Mk 3 20mm cannons were mounted in the nose section and were fed from four magazine boxes, two of which were located in the nose, and two of which were located under the cockpit. The gun carried 190, and later 170, rounds per gun. Overall, the Panther was considered to be a highly stable guns platform, owing in large part to the AN/APG-30 ranging radar unit. Panthers flew with full loads of 20mm ammunition on all flights unless configured for maximum range. (Northrop Grumman History Center)

The nose section is sheered off of this Panther as it lands aboard the Princeton. Early in the Korean War it was noted that exploding built-up gun gases caused some nose sections to sheer off. The Panther was designed with a sliding nose section mounted on rails so it could be removed or opened for maintenance of the electronic equipment or for cleaning or leading of the 20 mm guns in the nose. VF-91 found that after extensive use of the guns, the nose section would sometimes come unlatched and take off down the deck on carrier during landing. (Steve Ginter)

An external view of the nose section and internal studies shows the placement of the Panther's four 20mm guns. The guns presented problems—stoppage, jams, and broken links—for maintainers early in the Korean War, but those problems were worked out by war's end. Photo above left shows the two ammunition boxes on top as well as some of the electronics. (Northrop Grumman History Center)

Crews work with the AN-N6a gun camera mounted in the Panther's starboard wing. This camera operated with the gun to capture and record images so as to confirm aerial kills. (Northrop Grumman History Center)

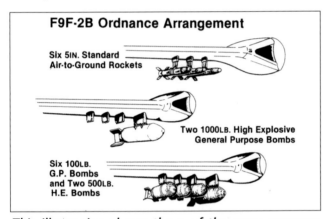

**F9F-2B Ordnance Arrangement**

Six 5IN. Standard Air-to-Ground Rockets

Two 1000LB. High Explosive General Purpose Bombs

Six 100LB. G.P. Bombs and Two 500LB. H.E. Bombs

This illustration shows three of the more common ordnance configurations used by the F9F-2B. (Published with the permission of Jim Sullivan)

Modifications made to the F9F-2B permitted the Panther to carry a variety of air-to-ground munitions. Here, three 5-inch HVARs are fitted to the Mk 9 Mod 0 launch rails. The small wires connecting the rockets to the wing provide the fusing. (Jim Sullivan Collection)

effective in starting fires, while the AP was excellent in destroying transportation vehicles or damaging tank tracks."[lviii]

Several problems developed with the Panther's gun system.[lix] After experiences during the early part of the Korean War, the Navy contacted Grumman and complained that pilots were experiencing nose-section separations after firing the cannons. It was believed that this phenomenon was caused by an accumulation of gun gases in the nose section, which then exploded, forcing the nose section to unlatch, move forward, and sometimes to eject. Although at first denying there was any problem, Grumman undertook a series of flight tests conducted at 35,000 feet using a spark igniter system, which failed to reproduce the problem. Test pilot Corky Meyer then asked to conduct a test flight, and on his first flight, succeeded in causing the explosion. It was later discovered that Grumman tests had used the igniter while the guns were being operated; Meyer had fired the guns, and then switched on the igniter, which reproduced the explosion. The end result caused a modification of the nose section, adding a series of small gun gas vents. Meyer's test flight also revealed that there was no way to ensure that the nose-section lock mechanism was actually engaged. As a result, Grumman modified the assembly with a small portal, allowing ground crews to view the locking mechanism and to ensure that the nose section was securely attached.

The Panther utilized an Mk 6 Aircraft Fire Control System (AFCS) (Mod 0 for rockets and Mod 1 for guns only), which was consisted of an Mk 8 Mod 0 sight unit mounted on a bracket on the cowl centerline, and an Aero 2C gun sight mounted just beneath. A gyroscope controlled the sight line to provide gun leads during high-speed engagements. Using this system, the pilot would simply aim the aircraft such that the gyro reticule image remained on the target, and then follow the sight line to the target until it was destroyed. An AN/APG-30 gun ranging radar unit was also provided in later models beginning with aircraft 123645, and incorporated into some earlier production units. Aircraft 122560 to 123083 did not have this equipment.

One problem experienced with the 20mm cannons concerned jams and stoppages. According to Action Reports from the Air Groups returning from Korea, the vast majority of the stoppages (some 67 percent) resulted from the hydraulic system used to charge the cannons for firing. This stoppage problem continued with the F9F-5 despite the fact that the Navy was involved in a war. After Action Reports show that Panthers were experiencing an average of one stoppage per 1,800 rounds, which given the Panther's 1,600-round capacity, meant that there was a failure on nearly every mission.[lx] As a point of reference, the failure rate for the .50-cal guns used on most Navy planes during World War II ran about one in 8,500 rounds.

Despite the stoppage problems, the 20mm was generally regarded as a good gun. One pilot, who flew the

F9F-2 during the Korean War, has said about the Panther's guns, "When they did fire, the jet makes an ideal platform for strafing, and getting good hits on a small target was not difficult. Only a few rounds were needed to severely damage or destroy a truck or ox cart."[lxi] Due to this effectiveness, many pilots elected to use only two of their four guns during strafing runs, so as to ensure they had ammunition on hand should they encounter enemy MiGs during their target egress. This was particularly true for missions north of Hamhung, which was well within the range of the Chinese MiG bases.

### The F9F-2B

Due to the pressing need for ground support during the Korean War, the Navy modified a number of F9F-2 as fighter-bombers, designating them F9F-2Bs, by adding four bomb racks under each wing. The inner rack was stressed to handle up to 1,000 pounds of iron bombs, with the outer three racks stressed at 250 pounds each, and could carry either 250-pound Mk 64 iron bombs or 5-inch HVARs.

*This image shows a nice view of the sliding canopy of the Panther. Here, a VF-831 F9F-2B (BuNo 127149) is loaded with four 250-pound GP bombs and is awaiting launch from the aircraft carrier* Antietam *in late 1951.* (Naval Aviation Museum)

This modification gave the F9F-2B Panther a maximum external load of 2,800 lbs; subsequent designs, namely the F9F-4 and F9F-5, had a capacity for 4,000 and 3,465 lbs, respectively, of external ordnance with empty tip tanks, but these weights were impacted by the type of catapult used for launch and whether the wingtip tanks were full. A Panther with full tip tanks had a 2,740-pound weight limitation when launched from the H8 and H4-1 catapults.

The pylons were added to all production F9F-2s commencing with aircraft 125083; once a majority of the F9F-2s were so fitted, the Navy dropped the –B designation and all reverted to simply F9F-2. VF-191, flying off of the carrier USS *Princeton* (CV-37), was the first squadron to deploy with the F9F-2B and on 2 April 1951 put them to use in a bombing attack against a North Korean railroad bridge near Songjin.

### Panther Weapons

Bombs were fitted to the inner wing stations using the Mk 51 Mod 0 bomb rack, while rockets were fitted to the three smaller stations using the Mk 9 Mod 2 Rocket Launchers. Bombs fitted on the outer stations used the Mk 55 rack. An AN/N6a gun camera was

*Navy Panther readies to launch carrying a small 100-pound General Purpose (GP) bomb and a single HVAR 5-inch rocket on each wing. The wing-folding mechanism was powerful enough to raise and lower the wings with no external weapons, but full wingtip tanks, at wind-across-deck at up to 52 knots. Moreover, it was likewise possible to fold and unfold the wings with six 500-pound bombs and full wingtip tanks, so long as wind-across-deck speed did not exceed 32 knots.* (Jim Sullivan Collection)

Pilot from NATC evaluates the weapons carriage of the F9F-2. Here, two 250-pound GP bombs are carried on each wing using the Mk 55 bomb rack. (Northrop Grumman History Center)

F9F-2 BuNo 123473 carries two 1,000-pound bombs during test flights to evaluate the Panther's ground attack capabilities. (Northrop Grumman History Center)

A modification of the HVAR, the Anti-Tank Aerial Rocket (ATAR) was used to strike North Korean armor. It was quickly discovered that the standard HVAR was not effective against the Soviet-built T-34 tanks used by the North Koreans and Chinese. A quick fix was developed at the NAS China Lake weapons test center and rushed into theater operations in October 1950. Here, two ground-crew personnel load a single ATAR onto a Marine Corps F9F. The ATAR featured a shaped-charge warhead that could penetrate the thicker Soviet armor. (Jim Sullivan Collection)

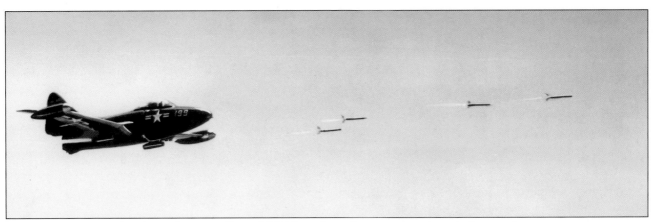

*A China Lake Panther launches a volley of FFAR rockets from underwing rocket pods on a weapons range at the famed Southern California desert test site.* (U.S. Navy via Gary Verver)

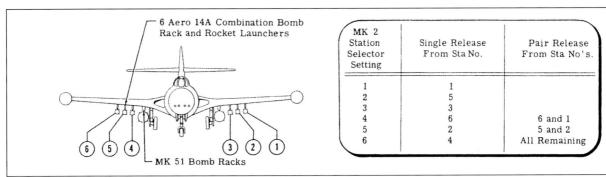

| MK 2 Station Selector Setting | Single Release From Sta No. | Pair Release From Sta No's. |
|---|---|---|
| 1 | 1 | |
| 2 | 5 | |
| 3 | 3 | |
| 4 | 6 | 6 and 1 |
| 5 | 2 | 5 and 2 |
| 6 | 4 | All Remaining |

*Schematic diagram shows the rocket-firing sequence for the F9F Panther.*

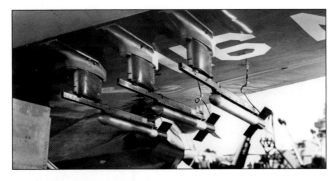

*This photo reveals the details of the 2.75-inch rocket assembly and the Aero-14A launch rail. One of the problems frequently encountered on the carriers involved the disconnection of the wires from the wing to the rocket during catapult launches. As a result, many rockets did not fire and had to be brought back to the carrier when the jets came aboard.* (Jim Sullivan Collection)

*A rear-view photo of the HVAR rockets on a Marine Corps Panther. Since they launched from land bases, Marine Panthers did not have the same take-off restrictions, as did those based aboard the carriers.* (Northrop Grumman History Center)

*Experiments at China Lake produced some interesting developments. Here, a collection of seven FFAR 2.75-inch rockets are contained in clear-plastic Shelly cluster launchers mounted on F9F-2 BuNo 127090.* (U.S. Navy via Gary Verver)

**A Marine Corps Panther from VMA-115 poses with two bombs and a single HVAR on each wing.** (Northrop Grumman History Center)

also mounted on a bracket in the right wing stub, which was operated by a switch on the armament panel, and keyed by the trigger switch, recording when the guns were fired. At the time, the primary iron bombs were the World War II vintage Mk 57 250-pound, Mk 64 500-pound, and Mk 65 1,000-pound bombs.

HVARs developed during World War II, were steel-encased 5-inch rockets that could reach a velocity of 1,375 feet per second and could penetrate 1½ inches of armor and up to four feet of concrete. It was used against ships, pill-boxes, fortifications, locomotives, vehicles, and tanks, and to suppress anti-aircraft batteries. Its warhead consisted of a Mark 35 common projectile with nose and base fuses and a 7.9-pound TNT charge. A more powerful version was also created for use against hardened targets, such as tanks, after it was discovered that the 5-inch HVARs were not effective against the Soviet-built T-34 tanks used by the North Korean and Chinese armies. Featuring a 6.5-inch-diameter shaped-charge warhead, these were called Anti-Tank Aerial Rockets (ATARs) and also referred to as RAM rockets. The ATARs were hastily developed at the Naval Ordnance Test Station (NOTS) China Lake in less than a month and rushed onto the battlefield in Korea.[lxii]

HVARs were fired using the gun sight, which proved very good for rocket launches. The pilot simply entered a dive and placed the center of the gun sight on the target. A slight counter-clockwise twist of the throttle activated the gyros controlling the rockets. The rockets were then fired once the aircraft reached a slant range of about 3,500 feet. HVARs were used primarily for attacks on rail lines, flak suppression, and against troops. Although highly effective when they worked, some air groups experienced problems with the electronic wire system used to arm the rockets. Because the rockets were designed in World War II, a time when there were no jets, the HVARs were not designed to take the abuse dished out by the higher speeds of jet operations. Thus, many rockets experienced broken electrical connections of the pigtail wire. Some air groups experienced as much as a five percent failure rate. This presented problems not only for the pilot, who unsuccessfully sought to launch the HVARs against an enemy, but also for carrier deck crews, who often had to deal with "hung" rockets, or rockets breaking loose upon catapult or arrested landing and skidding across the flight deck.[lxiii]

**The four wing pylons are clearly visible in this photograph of deck personnel refueling an F9F-2B.** (Northrop Grumman History Center)

Some Panthers, particularly those of the Marine Corps, carried the 11.75-inch Tiny Tim unguided rocket, which could be mounted only on the inner pylon. The rocket, designed by engineers at China Lake as a bunker-buster, had a range of approximately 1,640 yards and carried a 150-pound high-explosive warhead, which when combined with its velocity, had the explosive impact of a 500-pound bomb. A custom drop launcher was perfected for firing the Tiny Tim, which consisted of an Mk 51 bomb rack, a lanyard, and lanyard-operated switches. Like a bomb, the rocket was suspended from the bomb rack and fell away from the plane once released. As it fell, the rocket pulled out an 8-foot lanyard, which unreeled until two micro switches were actuated, igniting the rocket propellant. This launch system delayed firing of the rocket's motor until the Panther was safely out of the potential zone of rocket blast and, therefore, prevented damage to the aircraft from the rocket's exhaust.

Panthers also used the 2.75-inch (70mm) Mk 4 Folding-Fin Aerial Rocket (FFAR) fired from LAU-3/A 19-tube pods. These pods were carried on the aircraft's two inner pylons. Remnants of World War II, these rockets were originally intended to be used in the air-to-air role against enemy bombers, but they proved highly inaccurate. The FFAR was dubbed the "Mighty Mouse." VMF-115 was one of the first squadrons to test the new rockets in combat.[lxiv]

Panthers carrying external stores were subjected to certain operational restrictions. For example, aircraft carrying external stores were limited at altitudes above 5,000 feet to Mach .85 when carrying 100-pound bombs or HVARs and to Mach .77 when carrying 250-, 500-, or 1,000-pound bombs. Moreover, when carrying bombs fitted with the short, box-type fins, airspeed was limited to Mach .55, or about 350 knots. Pilots were also limited to four high-speed passes while carrying the box-type fin bombs. Maximum acceleration while carrying 500- or 1,000-pound bombs was restricted to 6.0 gs.

## The F9F-4 and F9F-5 Panther

The F9F-4 and -5 saw the introduction of heavier stressed outer wing stations, now increased to 500 pounds, and the Aero 14A Combination Bomb Rack and Rocket Launcher for use on the smaller pylons. However, each of the guns saw their ammunition decreased to 170 rounds, for a total of 760 rounds.

### Maximum Stores Weights

| Wing Pylon Rack and Rack (pounds) | Nominal Bomb Weight (pounds) | Combined Weight of Store |
|---|---|---|
| Mk 51 | 1,000 | 1,265 |
| | 500 | 646 |
| | 250 | 311 |
| Aero 14A | 500 | 605 |
| | 250 | 271 |
| | 100 | 131 |
| | 5-inch HVAR | 159 |

The maximum permissible bomb weight was 1,000 pounds on the Mk 51 rack and 500 pounds on each of the Aero 14A racks, with a total weight on 3,000 pounds. The armament panel featured a "safety" switch for each Mk 51/55 rack, a gun/HVAR selector switch, and a "dive angle" switch, selecting "35 degrees and over" or "35 degrees and under." A dial switch allowed selection of either a single rocket or release in pairs. The gun and bomb trigger was located on the control stick.

The new Aero 14A bomb racks presented problems for the Panthers deployed in Korea. As the USS *Princeton* Action Report noted:

*This VMF-115 F9F-2B has three HVARs on each wing.* (Northrop Grumman History Center)

"Difficulty has been encountered with the Aero 14A bomb racks in use on the F9F. The Aero 14A bomb rack suffered from design defects that affected loading, maintenance, and releasing bombs. In accordance with Task Force 77 directives, the racks are now disassembled after each malfunction and a report was made on the failure. It has been found that bent and broken sears are causing the trouble."[lxv]

The Action Report further noted:

"Aero 14A racks, while an improvement over the previous racks [used by the F9F-2], are generally not sturdy enough to stand up under the rigorous conditions that must be imposed upon them. Bombs up to, and including five hundred pounds, must be supported on taxiing aircraft with the wings in folded position, on cat-

A swept-wing F9F-6 Cougar (BuNo 127215) goes through weapons evaluations carrying a 1,000-pound bomb under each wing. The long red-and-white-striped nose boom was to record flight test data only, and was not part of the airplane's operational combat configuration. (Northrop Grumman History Center)

The F9F-8 (BuNo 141140) was the most formidable of the F9F series. The late-model Cougar served Navy fleet squadrons as both a jet fighter and attack aircraft. This Cougar carriers a drop tank on its inboard pylons, plus four AIM-9 Sidewinders—two on each wing. The nose probe pictured here was for inflight refueling. (Northrop Grumman History Center)

apult launches, and on arrested landings."[lxvi]

Unfortunately, solutions were not readily forthcoming from the Navy and it was not until February 1953 that the Aero 14B replaced the Alpha model.

Tests were also carried out on the F9F-5 with 150-gallon fuel tanks on the inboard weapons pylons. As a result, the inner pylons were made "wet" to permit more fuel carriage for longer-range missions. These were used largely on the F9F-5P.

## F9F Cougar Armament

Although the Cougar carried the same 20mm cannon as the Panther, the external weapons carriage differed in that Cougars had only two pylons per wing. The inboard pylon was rated at 1,000 pounds and was "wet," thereby permitting the carriage of 150-gallon fuel tanks. The outboard pylon was rated at 500 pounds. The two-seat F9F-8T Cougar, which was used largely for training, featured only two 20mm cannons, each with only 170 rounds. Two of the guns had been removed to help off-set the added weight of the additional cockpit.

The swept-wing F9F Cougar was capable of carrying the heat-seeking AIM-9 Sidewinder air-to-air missile, which had been developed in the early 1950s, and in fact was the first Navy fighter to deploy with the AIM-9. VA-46's Cougars made the first Sidewinder equipped deployment to the Mediterranean in 1956 aboard USS *Randolph* (CV-15). Although designed as a trainer, some of the two-seat F9F-8Ts were later retrofitted to carry Sidewinders as well. Other weapons were also used on the Cougars, most of which were not available at the time the Panthers flew operationally. As the 1950s progressed, new weapons such as the Mk 80 series low-drag bomb and Zuni rockets became available. The Mk 80s series bombs were created by Douglas Aircraft as a result of a study began in 1946 to evaluate lower-drag bomb designs to replace the larger General Purpose bombs of the World War II era. The Mk 80 series utilized the Aero 1A shape, which featured an 8:1 length-to-diameter ratio. The design was one of the many creations of Ed Heinemann, who designed the A-4 Skyhawk and other famous Douglas aircraft. Zuni rockets were developed in the early 1950s and were seen on Reserve Panthers and Cougars toward the end of the decade. The Zuni used a 5-inch (70mm) unguided folding-fin rocket fired from an LAU-10 four-tube pod. Zuni rockets were used for air-to-ground attack.

The F9F-8 had three wing stations, the innermost was "wet" and using the curved Aero 65A pylon could carry fuel tanks, bombs, or rocket pods. The two outer pylons could mount the Aero 15A bomb rack or an AIM-9 Sidewinder missile adapter and launch rail. The F9F-8 could carry two wing tanks and four Sidewinders, or two 1,000-pound bombs on the inboard bomb rack pylons and four 500-pound bombs on the four outer Aero 15A bomb rack pylons.

*Configured for an air-to-ground mission, this F9F-8 carried two 500-pound Mk 82s and a single 1,000-pound Mk 83 aerodynamic bomb under each wing.* (Northrop Grumman History Center)

### F9F-8B Low Altitude Bombing System (LABS)

A unique version of the F9F-8 was developed, designated the F9F-8B, and fitted with the Low Altitude Bombing System (LABS) for delivering "special" (i.e.,

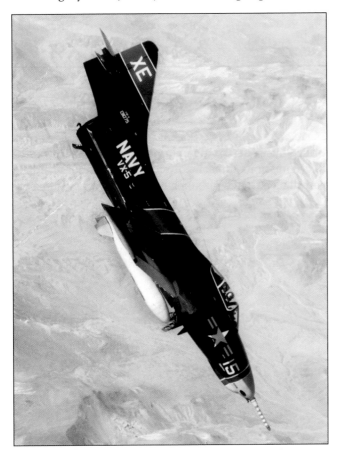

*A VX-5 F9F-8B (BuNo 131075) makes a dramatic dive while carrying a practice nuclear "special" weapon at one of the China Lake ranges. The bomb is a mock 12-kiloton (1,680-pound) Mk 7 carried on an Aero 22A bomb rack.* (U.S. Navy via Joel Aemselaar)

nuclear) weapons. LABS Cougars saw cockpit modifications, including the addition of a dive and roll indicator, an accelerometer, a horizontal yaw-roll gyro, a vertical gyro, and an ACS-Aero 18A or -22 bomb rack rated at 2,000 pounds. The LABS maneuver allowed for loft-bombing, where the attacking aircraft pulls upward just before releasing its bomb load, giving the bomb additional flight time by starting its ballistic path with an upward vector, and also allowing the pilot an opportunity to escape the blast effect. Loft or "toss" delivery methods included pop-up, level toss, dive toss, and over-the-shoulder. The Navy, rather than Grumman, handled all F9F-8B modifications. The F9F-8B deployed with many Navy squadrons and Marine Corps squadrons, including VMA-121, VMF-114, VMA-533, and VMFT-10, to name a few. Its nuclear role was assumed by other air wing aircraft, namely the A-4 Skyhawk and the larger twin-engine A-3 Skywarrior, and the A-5 Vigilante.

### Emerson Turret

Despite all of the benefits of jet propulsion, one of the drawbacks of jets is the speed at which engagements take place. The faster pace of combat meant that pilots had a shorter time window in which to use their guns to engage enemy aircraft. Although much research was underway on the development of guided rockets and missiles, such as the AIM-9 Sidewinder, forward-firing cannons were still the primary air-to-air weapon of the day. What was needed, it was thought, was some form of turreted cannon that could rotate with the passing aircraft and confront it in what was essentially an off-bore sight engagement, much like the turreted guns of bombers.

As a result of contracts let in mid-1949, experiments were conducted at NATC with the Emerson Electric quad .50 caliber turreted cannons mounted on an F9F-3 Panther (BuNo 122562). The four guns were supplied with 1,400 rounds of ammunition. The turret empowered

These two images capture the seemingly disastrous crash of Cdr. George C. Duncan while bringing his F9F-5 aboard USS Midway (CVB-41) during carrier suitability trials in July 1953. Miraculously, Cdr. Duncan survived the crash with only minor injuries, having been safely restrained in the cockpit, which separated cleanly from the aircraft after it hit the carrier's deck at a very high sink rate. (Jim Sullivan Collection)

Operationally, the F9F-4 and F9F-5 began entering service in late 1951. However, almost as soon as this occurred, both models began experiencing engine problems. These problems were so severe that all F9F-5s were grounded by late January. The F9F-4s, having experienced bearing problems, soon followed, and the Panther seemed in trouble. Grumman began working on the problem, and Pratt & Whitney redesigned a portion of the J48 engine. By June, all deficiencies were resolved and the new Panthers were back in squadron service. The F9F-4 and F9F-5's contribution to the Korean War effort is discussed later. However, at this point it is worth noting that all Panthers were quickly replaced by the high-performance swept-wing F9F-6 Cougar, which first flew in September 1951 and entered service at the end of 1952. Panthers were then assigned to the Auxiliary Training Units (ATUs) for use in jet training and transition, and in Composite Squadrons and Reserve units.

## Approach Speed Problems Lead to Wing Modification

Although the F9F-5 had passed carrier qualifications, word came from the Navy that the "F9F-5 stall speed must be reduced by 12 mph or they [would] be removed from carrier operations." Ironically, the solution came from prior observations made by test pilot Corky Meyer during his test flights. As Meyer explains in his book:

"During many of my flights in the F9F-5, I had been concerned about a large area of possible turbulent airflow behind the discontinuous intersection of the leading edge 'droop snoot' and the engine air ducts when the flaps and the droop snoot were extended as one for landing. To satisfy my curiosity, on one flight I had taped many 6-inch strings of yarn on the affected areas to visually note the airflow. I was amazed to see a large amount of turbulence, which extended to the trailing edge of the wing, and also the instant reversion to smooth flow when the flaps and droop snoot were retracted. The Panther aerodynamics people had pooh-poohed my supposition that lift was being lost because of the turbulence."[lxix]

Meyer went on to explain his solution:

"I now forced a piece of cardboard into the droop snoot slot at its inboard end, drew a fence outline for a template, had the resulting stiff aluminum fence installed and flight tested with our highly instrumented F9F-5 test aircraft."[lxx]

This photo shows the wing lock indicator it its raised position (center picture), and provide another view of the production-configuration wing fence. This was a slightly different shape and size from an earlier design. The intake's leading edge was also reshaped in later F9F-5s and retrofitted to earlier production models. (Jim Sullivan Collection)

Prior to actually landing a new aircraft type aboard an aircraft carrier for the first time, NATC conducts preliminary carrier qualifications at a naval air station on dry land. The F9F-4 and F9F-5 Panther were no exceptions. Here, F9F-4 (BuNo 125156) conducts landing gear tests at altitude before making its approach to NATC's land-based arresting gear facilities. (Northrop Grumman History Center)

An F9F-4 with its wings folded. In addition to the longer fuselage, the F9F-4 and -5, which were outwardly identical to one another, also featured a taller tail and slightly more pointed vertical stabilizer tip than earlier Panthers. (Jim Sullivan Collection)

Meyer's solution worked, knocking 9 mph off of the stall speed. Further modifications to the flap and wing fold hinge produced the final reductions needed to meet the Navy's demand.

As a result, a modification was made to the wing intakes of production aircraft 125907 through 126256 (and F9F-5P aircraft 126275 and subsequent), resulting in both a reshaping of the intake's leading edge (it now appeared as more of a horn or tooth) and the addition of a small wing fence just outboard of the intakes. The resulting change in airflow reduced the approach speed by 13 mph, which significantly enhanced safety during carrier landings. This modification proved so successful that it was added to many F9F-2s as well. Interestingly, Meyer continued working on the problem even after the modifications, and devised a means to reduce stall speed even further by replacing the F9F-5s droop snoot with a

*Spotting on the port and starboard catapults of the USS* Antietam *(CV-36), these Panthers from Air Group Fifteen are preparing to launch as soon as the crew of the Sikorsky HO3S (S-51) helicopter takes off on its life-saving "plane guard" patrol mission. These brave helo crewmen risked their own lives to rescue pilots who may have crashed into the water while either launching or "trapping" on the big carrier. These Panthers are assigned to VF-831 and VF-837.* (Robert Tallman)

set of experimental F9F-6 Cougar leading-edge slats. The resulting combination provided a further 11-mph reduction in stall speed without deteriorating the Panther's approach handling characteristics. This system, when combined with the Panther's water injection, would have given the F9F-5 the takeoff distance equivalent to that of the F8F-1 Bearcat. Meyer believed that this configuration, if adopted in the fleet, would have given the F9F-5 an additional 2,000 pounds of external ordnance capability.

## F9F-4 Boundary-Layer Control System

In an effort to generate more lift and reduce approach speeds, the 100th production F9F-4 (BuNo 125081) was modified during early 1954 to serve as a test bed for the high-lift Boundary-Layer Control System (BLCS) developed by John D. Attinello, a carrier suitability engineer at NATC.[lxxi] In theory, the system was to reduce the stall speed of the approaching aircraft by injecting high-speed air jets into the air stream to smooth the disturbed airflow over the deflected flaps. This additional jet air was to come from what was essentially "bleed" air from the engine compressor, which by its nature meant that there was less air powering the engine. Following wind tunnel tests that confirmed what Attinello had predicted, the modified F9F-4 was tested at NATC and then, in 1954, aboard USS *Bennington* (CV-20). The tests consisted of the following flights:

- 6 shore-based catapult launchings
- 21 shipboard catapult launchings
- 24 land-based arrested landings
- 20 shipboard arrested landings
- 8 shipboard touch-and-go landings

Another 20 flights were made to qualitatively evaluate the differences in aircraft performance and flying qualities with the super circulation system operative and inoperative.

*This F9F-4 Panther wears the ST markings, which means it flew with the Service Test Division responsible for evaluating the aircraft's operational and tactical suitability and maintenance.* (Steve Ginter)

*F9F-4 (BuNo 125156) wearing markings for the Flight Test (FT) Division, is seen here during carrier suitability trials in April 1954, which were conducted aboard USS Bennington (CV 20).* (Steve Ginter)

Modifications to the airframe were minimal, with a nozzle system fitted to the flaps of each wing and a collector added to the engine compressor to gather the bleed air. The tailpipe diameter was also increased from an effective diameter of 20.0 inches to 20.69 inches in order to maintain the necessary exhaust temperature (695 degrees C) when the bleed air was removed from the overall BLCS. According to report, the aircraft handled identical to a production F9F-4, except that it climbed more steeply and could land in a more nose-down position, which enhanced visibility.

While the system produced a reduction of 10 mph in stall speed, which meant that the aircraft could takeoff in 100 to 150 feet less distance, it was discovered that the F9F-4, equipped with the Allison J33-A-16 turbojet, was simply not powerful enough to maintain its altitude in the slower approach speed, even with full power applied. In fact, the resulting loss in thrust was in the range of 11 percent. Meyer has said in retrospect that the tests should have been performed on the F9F-5, which had the more powerful Pratt & Whitney J48 engine, and which would not have suffered the same performance degradation.

## Experiments With Aerial Refueling

Carrier-based jet aircraft of the early 1950s were limited by the fuel contained in their internal and wing tanks. In the summer of 1952, experiments were undertaken with a nose-mounted in-flight refueling probe to at least one F9F-5 (BuNo 125240) and testing was done using a North American XAJ-1 modified as a tanker and fitted with a drogue and reel. These tests were indeed so successful that the Navy announced in mid-1955 that all future jets would be fitted with some form of an external probe for in-flight refueling. This in-flight refueling probe later found its way into some F9F-6 and all F9F-8 Cougars.

## F9F-4 and F9F-5 General Facts

The F9F-4 had a range of 1,175 miles and an operational service ceiling of 44,600 feet. The aircraft had an empty weight of 10,042 pounds, which was just over 100 pounds lighter than the F9F-5. Given the strengthened wing pylons, the F9F-4 could carry an external load of 4,000 pounds. Initial deliveries of the F9F-5 began on 5 November 1950, and production continued through 13 January 1953. Production aircraft numbered 125081, 125156 through 125227, and 125913 through 125948. With its more powerful engine, the F9F-5 could reach a top speed of 604 mph at sea level with a standard combat weight and had a rate of climb of 6,000 feet per minute. Due to the more efficient J42-P, the F9F-5 had a range of 1,300 miles. It had an operational ceiling of 42,800 feet and an empty weight of 10,147 pounds. Both improved Panthers had a maximum takeoff weight of about 20,600

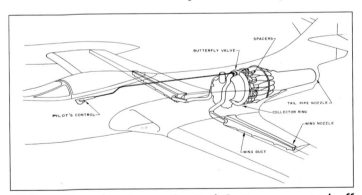

*The Boundary Layer Control System operated off bleed air from the Panther's engine. Corky Meyer, Grumman's primary test pilot during the Panther years, has commented that the system might have worked had tests been conducted using the F9F-5, with its more powerful J42-P-6 engine, rather than the underpowered F9F-4 and its J33-A-8.* (Northrop Grumman Corporation via Tommy Thomason)

*Right-hand console houses the aircraft's radios and navigational systems controls. The jet's white wing-folding handle is safely out of the way at extreme right.* (Jim Sullivan Collection)

As the Action Report concluded, during this dog-fight the MiGs were able to turn and maneuver with the F9F-5 "with apparent ease." Williams confirmed this in an interview for this book, stating that the MiGs appeared to turn with ease. However, he did not get an opportunity to fully experience the MiG's turning potential because the MiGs were traveling so fast, they simply over-shot him and maneuvered for a second pass.[lxxxv] "The fight was fought with the F9F-5 at a continuous 100 percent RPM." Yet, when the MiG wanted to break away, "he pulled away in a rapid, climbing turn to recover the advantage for another pass." As William's later put it, "the fight was largely in the horizontal" due to the overshooting.

The CAG 102 Action Report continued:

VF-781, a Reserve squadron, made a 1951 deployment to Korea aboard USS Bon Homme Richard (CV-31). The squadron flew the F9F-2B and was the sole Panther fighter squadron aboard. It was complemented by three F9F-2P photoreconnaissance Panthers deployed with VC-61 Det. G. (Northrop Grumman History Center)

This image features a nice profile of an F9F-2 from VF-831 aboard USS Antietam (CV 36) as it taxis toward the catapult for launch. (Naval Aviation Museum)

"Lt. (j.g.) Rowlands climbed to rejoin his section leader and the air battle turned into a melee. It may be that the three MiGs unaccounted for had now joined in the fracas. The pilot had extreme difficulty keeping track of the MiGs. As Rowlands reached the scene of action, a MiG made a head-on run, firing from far out and breaking sharply to the left in a steep climbing turn. With planes all around him, Rowlands found himself in an advantageous position with a MiG in his sights. Firing a long burst, he started it smoking but was diverted by another jet attacking him. The MiG and the F9F-5 ended up circling with neither jet gaining advantage. The MiG finally leveled his wings and climbed away rapidly.

Another MiG turned inside Williams and scored a hit, seriously damaging the F9F-5. A high-explosive shell severed rudder controls and knocked out the aileron boost. With the MiG still firing on his tail, Williams dove for a cloud bank 10,000 feet below him and approximately 10 miles away. Rowlands followed, although out of ammo by this time. He flew almost a loose wing position on the enemy jet in an effort to drive him off.

About this time Lt. (j.g.) John D. Middleton was vectored up to aid his two squadron mates. His indoctrination to aerial combat was a head-on by one of the swept-wing jets who came in from the two o'clock position. Lt. Middleton countered him and simultaneously saw Lt. Williams, a MiG, and Rowlands diving toward the cloud bank. As he dove to render aid, a MiG made another run on Middleton. On breaking away the enemy plane reversed course and apparently lost the F9F-5 in the sun, for he remained in perfect position for a 90-degree deflection shot. Middleton tracked him, fired from far out, and continued firing as the MiG's superior speed caused the Panther to tail in behind him. The pilot bailed out and Middleton saw the plane crash into the sea and the pilot land in the water.

Meanwhile, Lt. Williams and Lt. (j.g.) Rowlands reached the safety of cloud cover and after flying in the "soup" for about five minutes received a steer to the Task Force which was under the overcast. They made individual letdowns breaking out in the clear at 1,200 feet. The crippled Panther made a successful landing aboard followed by the other three Panthers."[lxxxvi]

As Lt. Williams' division landed, a second CAP division, lead by VF-781's skipper, LCdr. Stan Holm, was launched from *Oriskany* to protect against the MiGs' return. As the division reached its CAP station, Holm caught a glimpse of two MiGs disappearing to the northwest. Although it was not known at the time, the MiGs were actually Soviet fighters that had been launched from Vladivostok.

Meanwhile, Williams' experience for the day was not yet over. Due to communications and identification foul-ups, he was mistaken for an enemy aircraft when returning to his carrier and fired upon by the ships of Task Force 77. An alert watchman recognized the Panther and radioed "friendly." Williams then made a difficult landing aboard *Oriskany*. Due to his battle damage, he had little control over his Panther. Experiencing problems with his ailerons, and having only marginal elevator control, Williams made a two-handed landing, coming in at 170 knots, well over the standard 115 knots.

Reports from the debriefing indicated that the MiGs had no markings and radio intercepts confirmed that orders were being given in Russian, although Williams did not discover this fact for several years afterward. Officially, Lt. Williams and Lt. (j.g.) Middleton were credited with one MiG kill each and Lt. (j.g.) Rowlands was credited with a damaged MiG. Lt. Williams and Lt. (j.g.) Middleton each received the Silver Star and Lt. (j.g.) Rowlands received the Distinguished Flying Cross. *Oriskany*'s radar officer reported that at least five of the MiGs were either damaged or destroyed.

The Carrier Air Group Action Report concluded with an assessment of the engagement:

"It is felt that the success of what is believed to be the Navy's first jet dogfight with MiG-15s is attributable to the following factors:

(a) Defensive tactics developed and practiced by the Air Group in countering at the right moment when a high-speed jet is definitely committed to his run.

(b) Continual practice of a sound lookout doctrine.

(c) Aggressiveness of the pilots and their ability to fly the airplane to the maximum of its potentiality.

(d) The excellent performance of the 20mm guns and the APG-30 radar ranging gunsight.

(e) The seeming inexperience of these particular Communist pilots in their failure to take greater advantage of their high-performance aircraft."[lxxxvii]

Many years after the war, and after then Capt. Williams retired, it was revealed that he had actually scored at least three MiG kills that day. According to a story reported by Lyle E. Davis in *The Paper*, a North San Diego County newspaper, while Lt. Williams and his carrier skipper knew of the three kills, the National Security Agency, which had been conducting surveillance missions near the Soviet border and overheard the transmissions in Russian, wanted the information suppressed to protect their surveillance program.[lxxxviii] The MiGs belonged to the 781st IAP, 165th IAD, based near Vladivostok; the Soviet pilots killed were Capt. Belyakov, Capt. Vandalov, Sr. Lt. Pakhomkin, and Lt. Tarshinov. Unfortunately, the official Navy Action Reports have never been modified to reflect what really happened that day or to fully credit Capt. Williams with his full lot of kills.

No Navy F9F losses were sustained as a result of MiG-15 engagements, although one F9F-2 was heavily damaged in an engagement on 10 May 1952. An F9F-2B also engaged a MiG-15 on 21 July 1951 with no results.[lxxxix] Despite the Panther's perceived shortcomings against the swept-wing fighter, F9Fs went on to claim

roughly a half-dozen fighter aircraft in aerial engagements, demonstrating that the Panther, in the hands of capable pilots, could defeat a more sophisticated aircraft.

## Carrier Squadrons Adapt to the MiGs

Although each carrier air group dealt with the MiGs in different ways, Carrier Air Group Eleven (CAG-11) aboard *Philippine Sea* developed a comprehensive pamphlet, which it offered to the Chief of Naval Operations to distribute to new squadrons and ships operating the F9F-2. According to that pamphlet, "although the opportunity to conduct aerial combat against jet fighters has been limited to approximately five missions, several previous assumptions concerning tactics have been found to be in error."[xc] The report went on to explain these in more detail:

*Carrier crewman's view of F9F Panthers lined up on the flight deck of the USS* Antietam (CV-36) *preparing to launch for their next combat mission. This was a common sight during the Korean War, as seen from the carrier's port forward deck "catwalk."* (Robert Tallman)

*A snowstorm hits the Task Force 77 carriers in January 1952. Here, Panthers, Banshees, and Corsairs aboard the USS* Essex (CV-9) *wait out the weather to fly vital air strikes once again.* (Northrop Grumman History Center)

The Essex-class carrier USS Leyte (CV-32) made one Korean War deployment. Shown here was its sole Panther squadron, VF-31, which claimed a MiG-15 on 18 November 1951. Frederick C. Weber, who had been flying CAP for strikes over Sinuiji, flew that Panther. (Naval Aviation Museum)

### Single High-Speed Pass and Break-Away

The basic conception of combat in a jet fighter has previously been that due to tremendous speeds the firing time allowed would restrict tactics to a single pass and break-away for each plane of a division, and then a complete repositioning for a second attack. It was also thought that the evasive maneuvers of the attacked fighter would prevent any other than the single attack. Combat with the MiG-15 has proven otherwise, although it should be noted that without a single exception pilots rate the enemy pilots as poor, and it must be assumed that they did not fight their plane to best advantage. In the engagement with the MiG-15, no difficulty was experienced in gaining advantageous tail position, and holding this position for sufficient time to press an attack. The only evasive maneuver that could not be countered was the diving escape, but before this could be executed, ample attack time had been allowed. If the enemy jet could only resort to diving to escape, a successful encounter must be acknowledged, as friendly aircraft were safe from attack during this maneuver.

### Conventional Fighter Tactics Employed

The proven "scissors" tactics, as employed by conventional aircraft, were used to good advantage in gaining the offensive. The enemy jets that would stay in an encounter for any length of time were quickly confused and put on the defensive by "scissor" tactics.

### Altitude Advantages

Altitude advantages of more than a few thousand feet were found to be unsatisfactory because of the spotting problems. Unless below, or a little above, sight contact could not be gained, or maintained. However, this was not considered to be serious, as a jet fighter can stay at maximum speed in a level attitude, and the element of surprise is as great as when closing from below, or level, when commenced from the greater distances involved in jet versus jet combat, as it would be if a diving attack from altitude were used.

### Fuel

The theory that 100 percent power must be allowed for in computing time a jet fighter may remain in combat has been modified somewhat. It has been found that power ranges from 80 percent to 100 percent were used, and predominantly the lower percents until actual contact was made, and then power ranged from 90 to 100 percent, with 100 percent power used very little. Thus it was found that the jets could remain in the combat arcs considerably longer than the very short time planned for at first.

An F9F-2B landing aboard USS Antietam (CV 36) during 1951 operations off the coast of North Korea as part of Task Force 77. VFs-831 and -837 each deployed with 16 Panthers for the cruise. (Robert Tallman)

### Divisions or Sections

The employment of two-plane sections was found completely satisfactory against the relatively uncoordinated enemy jets; however the four-plane division should be used in cases of teamwork or coordinated attacks by the enemy.[xci]

These principles were based on the Air Groups' engagements, which included LCdr. Amen's 8 November MiG-15 kill.

Interestingly, it is not at all apparent that this pamphlet ever reached other squadrons, as is evidenced by George Schnitzer's comment in his book, *Panthers Over Korea*, "[It] was unfortunate that this document and others were never made available to the squadron. It would have been extremely useful in the event that our flight was attacked."[xcii]

A VF-721 F9F-2B Panther taxis to the catapult armed with two ATAR and one HVAR on each wing. This image shows the difference in size between the two rockets. (Northrop Grumman Corporation)

# CHEROKEE STRIKES

The brainchild of VAdm. J. J. "Jocko" Clark, Commander, Seventh Fleet, these strikes were a departure from the traditional close air support (CAS) and maximum effort strikes conducted by the Navy prior to mid-1952. While touring the theater in May 1952 shortly after taking command of the U.S. Seventh Fleet, VAdm. Clark conceptualized the basic nature of the so-called Cherokee Strikes after noticing how U.S. and UN ground forces were scattered about in the open near enemy lines.

"While flying behind our frontlines, I noticed many concentrations of our own forces that were not underground. These included supply concentrations, personnel housing, medical centers, truck parks, and ammunition dumps. As I flew over these areas, it occurred to me that if the enemy had the same air power and air supremacy that *we* enjoyed at the battle line, it would be impossible to have so much of our material freely exposed and in the open. I then reasoned that the enemy could not fight a kind of war he

was fighting and still have *all* his forces, supplies, and equipment underground. *Some* of his stocks of supplies had to be above ground, out of sight, and out of range of our artillery."[xciii]

Clark then ordered the carriers of Task Force 77 to fly reconnaissance over the areas in question, which confirmed his thoughts. As a result, the Navy launched strikes against these targets beginning in October 1952 and posted great success. Cherokee Strikes differed from traditional CAS, the former being pre-briefed, pre-arranged strikes, of heavy air power flown outside the bomb line. Weapons for the Cherokee Strikes were specifically chosen for their targets and jets were loaded with antipersonnel bombs for use in flak suppression. The strikes proceeded directly to the target in a coordinated group and once there conducted an immediate strike, minimizing time over target. The strikes were deemed very effective and welcomed by U.S. ground troops, who now faced a weakened enemy.

*Panthers from USS Boxer assemble to join an attack on port structures near Wonsan, North Korea, in July 1951.* (Jim Sullivan Collection)

## Panthers Move Some Mud

As the Action Reports from the aircraft carriers *Valley Forge* and *Philippine Sea* show, most of the F9F missions during the early months of the war focused on combat air patrols and escort, and air-to-ground attacks using the Panther's 20mm cannons. This, of course, was due to the fact that the Panther, as designed, was intended

*Braving the elements with snow on the ground, a Marine ground crewman checks the connections on the HVAR rockets of an F9F-2B belonging to VMF-311. The squadron was the first Marine Corps jet squadron to deploy to Korea, arriving in theater by early December 1950.* (Northrop Grumman History Center)

as a jet fighter and had no wing pylons for external weapons. The Panthers performed well in these roles; however, as the *Philippine Sea* Acton Report for the 1 November through 31 December period shows, one of the leading problems encountered arose from use of the 20mm cannon during cold weather. "The 20mm gun is one of the air groups [sic] greatest problems in the combat area during cold weather."[xciii] The Action Report continued, "It is considered that one of the main problems is the freezing of condensed water on the gun parts and on the ammunition trays and cans."[xciv] The guns were also plagued by belt breakages due to the Mk 7 20mm link.

The 1 November through 31 December Action Reports further elaborated on the escort tactics that had been formulated during the fall of 1950.

"In order to safely escort the conventional planes a new procedure was adopted by all jet squadrons of this Task Force. This consisted of establishing an approach and retirement corridor through which all conventional planes passed going to and returning from the target area. The initial point, designated Point Able, was set up over some well-defined landmark 30 to 40 miles from the objective area. Point Baker and Point Charlie were established as 1/3 and 2/3 of the distance toward the target. The strike leader informs the jet cover as he passes each of these points, to facilitate keeping track of the flight without having to constantly watch their progress. Usually four jet divisions were employed, with divisions stationed at 20,000, 25,000, 30,000, and 35,000 feet. A TARCAP

Coordinator is assigned each flight, and if cloud cover exists, he reassigns altitudes in the area. If the 35,000-foot level causes condensation trails, the division leader is free to lower his altitude, or with permission of the TARCAP Coordinator, he may become a roving division and assume any altitude. It has been found that short, one-syllable radio calls were a necessity while in the objective area."[xcv]

The Panther was clearly showing that it and its pilots were adapting to combat.

Indeed, the December 1950 Action Reports from the carrier *Leyte* (CV-32) confirm the Panther's initial limited fighter role. During the carrier's 49 days of air operations from 10 October through 25 December, the 16 F9Fs embarked with Air Group Three flew 821 sorties out of the 3,369 total sorties flown, and of these 207 were over Korea.[xcvi] F9Fs demonstrated a 77.7 percent availability rate, which was slightly below the 81.6 percent of the Air Group as a whole. F9Fs expended a total of 31,698 rounds of 20mm ammo, averaging 153 rounds per sortie, while not firing a single HVAR or Tiny Tim rocket, or dropping a single bomb.

Based on its experiences operating the F9F during the fall of 1950, the Action Report concluded that:

Jet planes assigned to the ship, although two less than a normal 18-plane squadron, were sufficient to meet scheduled demands of CAP, TARCAP, Sweeps, and condition 10 aircraft. It is recommended that the complement of jet aircraft for all CV-9 class carriers be limited to one squadron of 18 jet fighters. This is considered the most effective complement of aircraft for any operations foreseeable in the near future because it allows for the maximum number of attack type aircraft and yet provides an adequate jet defense for the Task Force and strike groups.[xcvii]

The *Leyte* operated a mix of 40 F4U and 26 AD attack aircraft.

### Enter the F9F-2B

Although the Panther remained the Navy's standard jet fighter throughout the war, the Panther's mission shifted from a pure fighter role to that of a highly

# CARRIER AIR GROUP COMPOSITION

The Carrier Air Group (CAG) provided the offensive punch for carrier forces. At the start of the war in June 1950, the U.S. Navy had seven attack carriers and nine carrier air groups, three of which were assigned to the Pacific. CAGs typically totaled 86 aircraft. Most of the carriers deployed during the Korean War operated with two fighter squadrons of 15 or 16 aircraft, usually of F9F Panthers, but on occasion of F2H-2 Banshees, two medium attack squadrons of 14 F4U Corsairs each, and a single squadron of 14 AD Skyraiders.

Each Air Group also possessed smaller detachments of two or three aircraft assigned special duties, such as photoreconnaissance, night fighter duties, night attack, and in some cases, electronic countermeasures (ECM) and airborne early warning (AEW). Together, these miscellaneous aircraft tallied another 14. Panthers were used in many of the photo detachments, as were F4U-5P Corsairs and F2H-2P Banshees. Variants of the Skyraiders, such as the three-seat AD-3N, AD-4N, and AD-4NL, were also used for night attack. The AD-2Q, AD-3Q, and AD-4Q was used for ECM and the AD-4W flew airborne early warning.

*VF-831 pilots aboard USS Antietam prior to launch. Note the flight gear, including helmets, goggles, "Mae West" life vests, and oxygen masks.* (Robert Tallman)

*Two reserve squadrons, VF-831 and -837, deployed with F9F-2Bs aboard USS Antietam (CV-36) during its sole Korean deployment from September 1951 through May 1952.* (Naval Aviation Museum)

VF-783 (which became VF-122) deployed aboard USS *Oriskany* (CV-34) as part of Carrier Air Group 102. As noted earlier, eight Navy fighter squadrons deployed with the F9F-5, which represented a significant improvement over the F9F-2. These squadrons included the following:

**F9F-5 Panther Carrier Deployments in Korean War**

| Deployment Date | Squadrons | Aircraft Carrier | Air Group |
|---|---|---|---|
| 15 September 1952 | VF-781 and VF-783 | USS *Oriskany* (CV-34) | CVG-102 |
| 20 November 1952 | VF-51 and VF-53 | USS *Valley Forge* (CV-45) | CVG-5 |
| 24 January 1953 | VF-153 and VF-154 | USS *Princeton* (CV-37) | CVG-15 |
| 30 March 1953 | VF-111 | USS *Boxer* (CV-21) | ATG-1 |
| 20 April 1953 | VF-111 | USS *Lake Champlain* (CV-39) | CVG-4 |

# CARRIER STATIONS

Major carrier operations during the Korean War fell under the command of the U.S. Navy Seventh Fleet. Central to these operations was Task Force 77, which maintained stations in the Sea of Japan (East Coast Task Force) and the Yellow Sea (West Coast Task Force), and provided air support and interdiction missions for United Nations (UN) ground troops on the Korean Peninsula. The larger U.S. carriers deployed in the Sea of Japan, while the smaller U.S. escort carriers, Royal Navy, and Royal Australian Navy carriers deployed in the Yellow Sea as part of Task Force 95. Some have said that the latter was due to the U.S. desire to not provoke the Chinese by having a large carrier presence off its shores.

When the war broke out in June 1950, Task Force 77 was centered on the U.S. carrier USS *Valley Forge* (CV-45) and embarked Carrier Air Group Five. In late June, it was joined by HMS *Triumph* (R. 16) with her 40 aircraft and 10 escorts. CVG-5 featured VF-51 and VF-52, operating F9F-3 Panthers, VF-53 and VF-54, flying F4U-4 Corsairs, and VA-55 flying the AD Skyraider. The Task Force launched its first strikes against North Korea on 3 July, a day after U.S. Army forces entered Korea in support of UN efforts, striking communications and transportation targets in and around the capital Pyongyang. The *Valley Forge* was joined in early August by *Philippine Sea* (CV-47), in September by USS *Boxer* (CV-21), and in November by USS *Leyte* (CV-32). USS *Princeton* (CV-37), which entered the region in December and replaced *Valley Forge*, maintained the number of fleet carriers deployed off Korea to four.

At any one time, three fleet carriers would be assigned to Task Force 77—two carriers would be conducting strike operations while the third conducted replenishment at sea. A fourth carrier would be in port in Japan, available on 12-hours' notice.

By war's end, 11 fleet carriers, all of the *Essex* class, would deploy with Task Force 77, making a combined total of 25 deployments. All but three carrier deployments included at least one F9F squadron in its embarked air group. A total of 16 aircraft carriers were reactivated and recommissioned to expand the carrier fleet and accommodate the demands of the Korean War deployments.

*The US Navy carriers operated from several locations off the coast of North Korean, as* indicated here by the two small circles, one in the Yellow Sea and the other in the Sea of Japan. TF 77 typically launched strikes from a position in the Sea of Japan, just north of the DMZ. (Matt Shepherd)

During its 28 October 1952 through 22 April 1953 deployment period, Air Group 102 flew a total of 7,001 flights and 14,948 flight hours during its 73 scheduled operational days. The F9F-5 Panther was used heavily in the attack role, including flak suppression and bombing:

"The F9F-5 type aircraft utilized as a bomber on many occasions proved to be a potent weapon. The bomb load carried was as much as 2,500 pounds of bombs per plane, using the Mk-8 catapult for launching. Four F9F-5 airplanes of VF-122 [VF-781], carrying two 1,000-pound bombs, attacked the heavily defended Hamhung Bridge and scored six hits out of a total of eight bombs dropped, making three large, complete cuts in the bridge."[cv]

## Summary of Flights

| Mission | VF-781 | VF-783 | Total Air Group |
|---|---|---|---|
| *Offensive* | | | |
| Strike | 479 | 463 | 2,617 |
| Recce | 307 | 314 | 621 |
| Flak Suppression | 152 | 157 | 309 |
| Photo Escort | 115 | 105 | 220 |
| Sweep | 8 | 7 | 15 |
| Strike Escort | 4 | 4 | 8 |
| Total | 1,126 | 1,105 | 5,040 |
| | | | |
| *Defensive* | | | |
| CAP | 509 | 524 | 1,039 |

In total, the two Panther squadrons each made 1,702 sorties, with an average of 68 flights per pilot and 104 (VF-781) and 105 (VF-783) average flight hours per pilot. VF-781 posted an 87 percent availability rate while VF-783 posted an 85 percent rate.[cvi]

*Princeton*'s F9F-5s were also used heavily in the strike role during a portion of its 1953 deployment. Its two F9F-5 squadrons flew 1,050 of the air group's 1,116 strike sorties during the 9 June through 3 August 1953 period, and flew 1,930 of the air group's 3,421 total sorties.[cvii] Of these, the air group's F9F-5Ps flew 103 photoreconnaissance sorties (with only 2 aborts), 88 of which were escorted. The Panther's primary missions included CAP (287), Recco (485), Strike (1,040), and Escort (88). On 15 June 1953 VF-154 set an air group record 54 sorties in a single day. VF-153 logged a 96.6 percent availability rate, while VF-154 hit 95.2 percent. VC-61's F9F-5P posted a 96.5 percent availability rate.

F9F-2s and F9F-5s made only one mixed deployment, that being on the USS *Boxer* (CV-21) in late 1953. On that cruise, VF-52 and VF-151 deployed with 14 F9F-2s each and VF-111 was later transferred into the Air Group with 16 F9F-5s, in exchange for VA-44, which transferred to USS *Lake Champlain* (CV-39). Most of the missions flown by the *Boxer*'s F9Fs were CAP, recce, or photo escort.

### "Papa Papa" Panthers

The Korean War also saw the introduction of the F9F-2P and F9F-5P photoreconnaissance aircraft, which were the Navy's first carrier-based jet-powered photo-recon planes. Throughout the war, photo Panthers routinely flew with VC-61 in two- or three-plane detachments and were quite active in gathering images. It was generally established that the F9F-2P represented "an improvement over prop-driven aircraft" in large part due to the aircraft's high speed and minimal vibration.[cviii] As the Action Report from *Princeton* shows, from 5 December 1950 through 10 August 1951 VC-61 Det. F9F-2Ps took and processed 11,128 aerial negatives and 5,390 still negatives, and generated 157,120 prints. The total gun camera and other 16mm film processed measured 63,000 feet.

Photoreconnaissance was used for a variety of purposes; at least one carrier utilized the Panther's photo services to prepare flak mosaics for distribution to task force carriers. As the USS *Essex* Action Report for 13 December 1951 through 3 February 1952 shows, "These mosaics were prepared for the major strikes as well as routine rail cutting and were well received by the Air Groups embarked."[cix] Photo Panthers were designated with "PP" tail codes, which distinguished them from other air wing aircraft. The F9F-2P flew with VMJ-1 starting in 1953, providing photoreconnaissance for the Marines.

*An aerial view of USS* Antietam *(CV-36) during its Korean deployment shows the size of its air group, which included two F9F-2B squadrons and several F9F-2Ps in the VC-61 detachment.* (Robert Tallman)

During December 1951 through March 1952 of USS *Essex* and CVG-5's deployment, two F2H-2P aircraft supplemented the F9F-2P detachment and were well received largely due to the effectiveness of their reconnaissance cameras.

"Two F2H-2P photo aircraft were ordered to this group during the operating period and were found to be a great improvement over the F9F-2P because of the types of cameras installed. The F2H-2P has one (1) K-38 camera with a 36-inch focal length and two (2) K-17s, one with a 12-inch focal length and one with a 6-inch focal length. The F9F-2P has two (2) K-17s with 12-inch focal lengths."[cx]

VC-61's detachment flew 95 total missions during the last period (December 1951 and January 1952), of which the F2H-2P flew 24 missions. The two F2H-2Ps stayed with the Air Group for the final period, from February to March, and together flew 34 missions.

## Marine Corps Panther Operations

The Marine Corps also operated the Panther, flying all models at some point during the war. Panthers were deployed with VMF-311 beginning in December 1950, which by month's end had logged over 400 combat hours. Twenty-four F9F-2Bs arrived in Yonpo (K-27) and then moved to Pusan (K-9) and provided air superiority, close air support, and reconnaissance for local ground troops. On 21 July, three VMF-311 Panthers were attacked by 15 MG-15s, and one pilot, 1st Lt. Robert W. Bell, was shot down. More MiG engagements followed in September and October, but the squadron suffered no more air-to-air losses. One VMF-311 Panther, aircraft 123451, held the honor of being the oldest combat Panther in Korea, having flown over 1,000 combat hours and expended over 400,000 rounds of ammunition, wearing out 16 20mm cannon barrels. The squadron received F9F-5s in 1953.

VMF-115 deployed to Korea in early 1952, basing at Pohang (K-3). The squadron operated a mix of F9F-2 and F9F-4 aircraft and tallied some impressive totals. For example, in December, the squadron set a personal record of 726 sorties despite heavy winter weather, which was then shattered in April 1953 with the squadron flying 1,392.2 combat hours. The squadron received 18 new F9F-5 Panthers in late April. In total, VMF-115 flew 9,250 combat sorties in 15,350 flight hours during their deployment.

LTJG Walter Spangenberg flew F9F-2 Panthers during the Korean War with VF-91 as part of Air Group Nine. His personal accounts can be found on pages 60-61, and 110. (Courtesy of W. Spangenberg)

The tail damage to this VF-831 F9F-2B is testimony to the damage a Panther could withstand and still stay controllable in the air all the way back to the ship. (Robert Tallman)

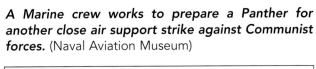

This VMA-311 photograph shows how engines were easily removed from Panthers using a small mobile hoist. (Northrop Grumman History Center)

A Marine crew works to prepare a Panther for another close air support strike against Communist forces. (Naval Aviation Museum)

VMF-311 was based north of Pusan for much of the war and provided strikes in support of frontline forces. Large-tire vehicles neatly lined up on the Pierced Steel Planking (PSP) ramp are bomb-loading carts for the jets' lethal payloads. (Northrop Grumman History Center)

VMA-311 ground-crew personnel refuel an F9F-2B's wingtip tanks and have already armed the aircraft for its next mission. This was a much easier task for Marine refuelers than for their U.S. Navy brethren. Those crewmembers had to perform this same duty high atop the flight deck of aircraft carriers with ladders to reach the tip tanks when the Panthers' wings were folded for deck storage. (Naval Aviation Museum)

## Famous F9F Pilots

The Korean War effort saw many participants who would go on to great fame in other areas of life, and the air war fought by Navy and Marine Corps pilots was no exception. During the war, three men whom we now regard as celebrities flew versions of the F9F Panther in combat—baseball legend Ted Williams, and future astronauts John Glenn and Neil Armstrong. Ted Williams was no stranger to the Armed Services. Williams enlisted with the Navy on 22 May 1942 and joined the V-5 program to become a naval aviator. He received his wings and commission in the U.S. Marine Corps on 2 May 1944. Known for his mastery of gunnery, Williams set many records during his flight training and upon graduation, obtained a slot as an instructor at NAS Pensacola, Florida. When the war ended, Williams was stationed in Hawaii awaiting orders to deploy to the waters off China. Williams was released from the service in January 1946 and returned to baseball, but remained in the Reserves.

However, when the Korean War broke out a few years later, the services found themselves woefully short of pilots and began recalling Reserve units in all branches. On 1 May 1952, Williams was recalled for active service and was assigned to the 33rd Marine Air Group (MAG-33). Williams completed his refresher training and was assigned to fly the F9F Panther, eventually being deployed with VMF-311 at K-3 airfield in Pohang, Korea.

Williams joined the squadron on 16 February 1953, and took part in a 35-plane strike against a North Korean tank and infantry factory near Kyomipo just south of Pyongyang. According to the description of the mission listed on his Web page, Williams was approaching his target, a troop encampment, at low altitude when he lost sight of the plane in front of him.

"He dropped down to regain visual contact, but went too low. North Korean soldiers in the encampment blasted him with small arms fire. He completed his run over the target and tried to pull up. Every warning light in the cockpit was lit and the plane was vibrating. The stick started to shake and he knew he'd sprung a leak in the hydraulic system."[cxi]

Immediately the landing gear came down and the aircraft shook and became hard to control. Williams managed to get his gear back up and pulled back on the stick, trying to climb. Williams then tried his radio and found it dead, which meant that he also could not hear all of the radio calls from his wingmen who were trying to tell him to bailout because his plane was on fire.

As his Panther continued to climb, Williams realized that he was in trouble and began a turn toward the nearest air base. By this time, most of his flight instruments were out and he was unable to raise of lower his flaps or lower his landing gear due to the lack of hydraulics.

Williams' fellow pilots were busy trying to motion for Williams to eject. When he refused, Lt. Larry Hawkins moved his F9F into the lead and lead Williams back to the field.

As he approached the field, the Panther continued to burn, trailing smoke from the brake ports and from a wheel door that had blown loose. Unable to slow his burning aircraft, Williams made his final approach at nearly 225 mph, almost twice the F9F's normal landing speed. In a moment his Panther struck the ground, sparks and fire trailing the aircraft as it scooted along the field. After a run out of nearly a mile, the Panther finally came to a stop, and Williams popped the canopy, diving onto the tarmac where Marines rushed him away. The Panther was completely consumed in flames and was a total loss.

Ted Williams had another close call two months later when his Panther was hit by anti-aircraft fire while on a low-level strafing run. During his time in Korea, Williams flew 39 combat missions and was regarded as an excellent pilot. He was eventually discharged in July 1953 due to an inner ear imbalance and returned to play baseball with the Boston Red Sox.

John Glenn flew the Vought F4U Corsair during World War II while stationed in the Pacific Theater. Glenn had originally signed up for the Army Air Corps just after Pearl Harbor; but when he did not get called to duty in March, he enlisted in the Navy as an aviation cadet. Glenn was then assigned to the Marine Corps and began flying with VMJ-353 flying R4D transports. After a short while, he obtained a transfer to VMF-155 and flew 59 missions as a Corsair pilot, seeing action in the Marshall Islands, and eventually being assigned to NAS Patuxent River, Maryland, where he was promoted to Captain and worked as a test pilot.

Glenn had a number of duties after the war, and when the Korean War began, he was flying the F9F Panther with VMF-311. While with VMF-311, Glenn served as section leader to Ted Williams and was with Williams during the 16 February mission described above. Glenn flew 63 combat missions during the war as a member of VMF-311 and another 27 missions as an exchange officer flying the F-86 with the Air Force. In that capacity, Glenn shot down three MiG-15s. After the war, Glenn became a test pilot and then was selected to enter the Project Mercury space program as one of the original "Mercury Seven" astronauts. Glenn was the fifth person in space and on 20 February 1962, became the first American to orbit the Earth.

A second famous astronaut also flew Panthers in the Korean War. Neil Armstrong, who would later be the first pilot to land on the moon, received his naval aviator's wings on 12 August 1950 and was assigned to Fleet Aircraft Service Squadron 7 (FASRON 7) at NAS San Diego (now known as NAS North Island). Two months later, Armstrong was reassigned to VF-51, flying the F9F-2B Panther. Armstrong made his first flight in the

This illustration shows a scene from the classic William Holden movie Bridges of Toko-Ri, which really featured the Grumman Panther in the starring role. (Northrop Grumman History Center)

Panther on 15 January 1951 and six months later, completed his first jet carrier landing aboard USS *Essex* (CV-9). Almost immediately thereafter, the squadron deployed to Korea as part of Carrier Air Group Five.

Armstrong's first taste of combat came on 29 August 1951 when he provided armed photoreconnaissance escort for one of the Air Group's F9F-2Ps. The targets for that mission were freight yards and a bridge south of the village of Majon-ni, just west of Wonsan. Five days later, Armstrong was making a low-level bombing run during a mission when his Panther (BuNo 125122) was struck by enemy anti-aircraft fire. The Panther took a quick nose dive and in so doing, sliced through a cable strung about 500 feet across the valley, shearing off a 6-foot portion of his right wing. Air Group Five's Action Report described this further:

"He lost elevator control, but in a fraction of a second he rolled-in all the back [trim] tab he could get. His aircraft, well loaded with ordnance, came so close to the ground that he sheered off two feet of his starboard wing on a power pole. By baying the stick and the trim tabs he was able to fly to friendly territory and to safety."[cxii]

Although Armstrong was able to nurse the damaged Panther back to friendly territory, the battle damage was so severe that landing was completely out of the question. He ejected over water, hoping to settle into the sea and be rescued by a Navy helicopter, but his chute drifted in the wind and forced him back overland. He was rescued by U.S. troops. Always exhibiting the cool "grace under pressure" quality that allowed him to survive emergency situations in the F9F, and later in the experimental X-15 rocket plane and Gemini space vehicle, Armstrong flew a total of 78 missions and 121 flight hours during the Korean War.

### Parting Thoughts

In all, the Panther played a leading role in the Navy's air operations in the Korean War. Not only is this apparent from the large number of missions flown by Panther squadrons, but from the number of deployments made

A VF-721 F9F-2B makes a run at a target in North Korea. The aircraft was flying from the USS Boxer at some point during the carrier's 1951 deployment. (Northrop Grumman History Center)

by Panther squadrons. Yet, despite the Panther's heavy usage, the F9F suffered a relatively low number of losses.

This low rate, 16 percent of major combatant losses, is surely a testament to the rugged construction of the Panther and the skill of its pilots in bringing them back to the carrier. Perhaps this is what was meant by Alan Bedford in his 1999 article on the Panther's operations in the Korean War, when he said, "[a]s with most Grumman products, it was mighty strong. They don't call Grumman the 'Iron Works' for nothing."[cxiii]

### U.S. Navy Carrier Aircraft Losses During the Korean War

| | | | |
|---|---|---|---|
| F2H Banshee | 15 | AD Skyraider | 211 |
| F4U Corsair | 555 | F3D Skyknight | 7 |
| F9F Panther | 163 | F7F Tigercat | 28 |

# WALTER SPANGENBERG'S OBSERVATIONS FROM KOREA

"Our missions with the F9F-2 were an assortment of combat air patrol (CAP), road, and railroad reconnaissance looking for trains or trucks that we very seldom found, flak suppression for strike aircraft when the target was not beyond our fuel range from the ship, and photo escort for the F9F-2P photo planes that were now part of our air wing. There was also a mission designated a 'Cherokee Strike,' on which we flew over the beach and checked in with an Air Force radar controller who then vectored us to a pre-selected location and ordered a bomb drop on his command. All this at a level 20,000 feet or so with 250-pound bombs probably did not do more than disturb some North Korean's morning nap. We liked to think of ourselves as fighters, but with limited performance we were really fighter-bombers, and left the MiG hunting to the Air Force F-86 pilots. We didn't really carry much of a bomb load either; perhaps six 250-pound bombs or an equivalent load of rockets on a cold day—less in warm weather when the ship had to make all of its own wind over the deck for takeoff. We did have four 20mm guns with 200 rounds of ammo each, and those were probably our best weapons for the air-to-ground work we did. The projectiles would explode on impact and did a pretty good job of damaging railroad tracks.

"Regarding the railroad recce missions, another thrill experienced by several Panther pilots was to have the airplane's sliding nose section forward of the windshield either vanish in a strafing run, or unlatch and open so that on shipboard arrestment it left the aircraft and went zooming down the deck, to the consternation of all observers the first couple of times it happened. This problem was traced to the lack of vent louvers to exhaust gun gas from the nose section, so that one was soon put to rest also. We were by no means the first Panther squadrons in Korea, but we may have been the first to use the guns in road and railroad reconnaissance enough to encounter this problem."

# CHAPTER SEVEN

# THE SWEPT-WING COUGAR ARRIVES

*Dramatic close-up of the third production F9F-6 Cougar (BuNo 156259) shown in flight. Note the natural extension aft of the F9F-5 Panther's leading-edge wing fences. Upper fuselage engine blow-in doors have been retained.* (Northrop Grumman History Center)

The Navy had been interested in swept-wing fighter designs since Allied forces obtained working examples of the German Me-262 at the end of World War II.[cxiv] Indeed, the Germans had successfully developed and deployed the advanced jet fighter in mid-1944 and had undertaken fairly extensive research into the benefits of swept-wing designs, specifically that of 35 degrees.[cxv] Swept-wing designs were generally superior to a straight-winged aircraft because the former permitted a higher Mach number. A swept-wing design appears thinner than a straight wing because the chord relative to the airflow is greater, which reduces transonic drag.

As early as 1946, the U.S. Navy, which had been charged with the responsibility of researching the low-speed stability behavior and stall characteristics of the swept-wing design, solicited industry bids for the development of a flying test bed to evaluate the flight performance of the swept-wing design. Grumman and Bell responded to this request; Grumman offered the design studies based on a modified F4F and also a new design, called Design 77, while Bell offered a variant of its propeller-driven P-63C5 Kingcobra. The Navy, acting through BuAer, awarded an experimental contract to Bell Aircraft to develop the L-39, largely due to the lower costs associated with building on a proven airframe. Two examples were produced, L-39-1 and L-39-2, each with wings swept back at 35 degrees, and adjustable leading-edge slats and trailing-edge flaps. The L-39 featured a short unswept inboard section that was employed to maintain the aircraft's center of lift. The two prototypes were identical except that L-39-1 possessed thicker flaps, which therefore produced a 56 percent larger slot.

Aircraft L-39-1 first flew on 23 April 1946 and after numerous modifications to it and L-39-2, the Navy was convinced that swept-wing design could be successfully used aboard carriers. Indeed, the Navy's Fighter Class Desk Officer, Cdr. A. B. Metsger, who himself was a former test pilot, even flew the aircraft in June 1946 and made several simulated carrier approaches. By August, the experimental flights had concluded and it was clear that the Navy would now move in the direction of swept-wing designs. It was these flights and the conclusions from the L-39 program that had given Cdr. Metsger the notion to include in the Panther contract at least preliminary design studies into a swept-wing F9F variant. Of interest to this book, one of the test pilots given the opportunity to fly the L-39 was Grumman's Corky Meyer.

### Grumman's Swept-Wing Design Efforts

Grumman had been conducting its own experiments with swept-wing designs. As noted earlier, Grumman had responded to the Navy's 1945 Request for Proposal with its Design 77, which was a low-wing design powered by a 450-hp Pratt & Whitney R-985 radial.[cxvi] Although the proposal was to feature a wing box structure arranged to accommodate wings with various degrees of sweepback, the flight characteristics and performance specifications for the 35-degree sweep called for a 24-foot wingspan with 210 square feet of area, and a maximum speed of 220 mph at sea level.

The Navy's rejection of the swept-wing proposals, which would have provided the company with a wealth of data concerning swept-wing flight, was one of the principle reasons that Grumman persuaded the Navy to postpone work on the swept-wing derivative of the Design 79 (XF9F-2) until it could have sufficient means to address from an engineering standpoint the poor low-speed attributes of the swept-wing design. At about the same time, Grumman began preliminary work on another swept-wing aircraft, Design 83, which eventually became the XF10F-1 Jaguar, and which further produced a Navy Letter of Intent in December 1947.[cxvii] The Jaguar was revolutionary in that it sought to incorporate a variable-sweep design. Meanwhile, the U.S. Air Force began development of its first swept-wing fighter, the North American XP-86, which flew for the first time in October 1947, and would become the F-86 Sabre.

### Navy Swept-Wing Efforts Pre-Korea

Given the level of activity taking place between 1948 and 1952, there is little question

*Grumman proposed two experimental swept-wing designs: one based on the F4F Wildcat and the second, a new design. Both were rejected by the Navy in favor of a swept-wing version of the P-63 offered by Bell Aircraft.* (Northrop Grumman Corporation; redrawn by Matt Shepherd)

The prototype F9F-6 Cougar (BuNo 126670) followed in trail by an F9F-5 Panther chase plane. The Cougar first flew on 20 September 1951 piloted by Grumman test pilot Fred C. Rowley. (Northrop Grumman History Center)

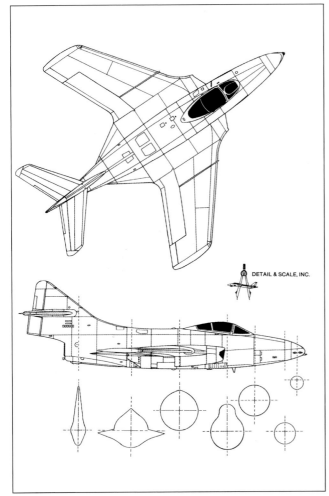

Plan view and right profile view show the classic lines of the swept-wing Cougar. (Bert Kinzey, Detail & Scale, Inc.)

that the Navy appreciated the importance of getting a capable swept-wing fighter design aboard carriers as soon as possible. Rumors had been circulating since 1948 that the Soviet Union had produced a swept-wing fighter, the MiG-15, which was seen in significant numbers at air shows during 1949. As has been noted in the aviation literature of that time period, the lack of a simple swept-wing jet-powered day fighter was not due to the aviation industry:

"It was certainly not a lack of initiative on the part of the Navy's aircraft contractors. Vought unsuccessfully suggested a swept-wing version of the F6U as a quick way to achieve high performance. McDonnell did design studies of a swept-wing variant of the F2H Banshee in 1947 that incorporated features from its Army Air Force F-88 design, including afterburners, but didn't get a contract modification to proceed."[cxviii]

This can perhaps be explained by the Navy's view of its mission at the time:

"The Navy did not have a dog-fighting, simply equipped, swept-wing aircraft in November 1950 [when the first MiG-15s appeared over Korea], because its focus was on defending the battle group against high-speed, high-altitude bombers with interceptors, and escorting medium-range, carrier-based bombers to the target in all weather conditions. As a result, the jet fighter programs initiated in the late 1940s after the F7U start were either short-range, fast-climbing, all-weather, rocket-armed, point-defense, bomber-destroyers, or big general-purpose fighters. A simple (e.g., no search radar), lightweight fighter did not fit into these plans."[cxix]

Even so, none of the Navy programs under consideration at the time were slated to fill that role, or even to be available until 1951. For the Navy, now faced with a high-performance, swept-wing jet adversary in the skies over Korea, the solution came in the modification of a proven product, the F9F Panther.

### The F9F-6 Cougar

On 3 March 1951, Grumman was awarded their second government contract calling for the development of a swept-wing jet fighter design based on the original Panther configuration. The contract came in large part as a result of the introduction of the swept-wing Soviet MiG-15 into the air war over North Korea. While the Air Force's F-86 was doing remarkably well in dogfights against the Communist adversary, the Navy was left with a collection of straight-winged fighters, such as the Panther, Banshee, and FJ-1 Fury, which simply could not

An excellent overhead view of aircraft 126670 just prior to its first flight shows the 35-degree wing sweep and larger overall wing surfaces of the Cougar. Notice the lack of wing fences on the early prototype. (Jim Sullivan Collection)

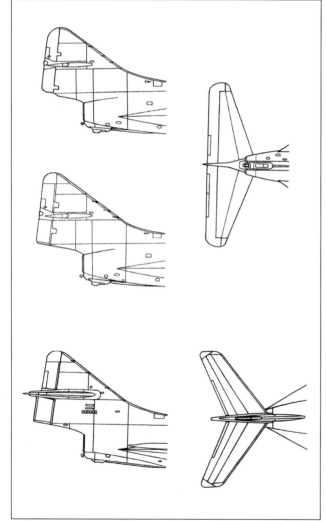

The rudders and aft tail section changed between the various models. The F9F-4 and -5 Panther had a taller rudder than the F9F-2 and -3, while the -6 Cougar and beyond incorporated the sweptback "flying tail" design. (Bert Kinzey, Detail & Scale, Inc.)

match the MiG-15's performance. Moreover, the FJ-2 swept-winged version of the Fury lacked the range to operate from carriers, given the distances involved.

Grumman responded by pulling three of its planned F9F-5 Panthers from the production line and modified them to serve as the XF9F-6 prototypes (BuNos 126670 and 126671) and static airframe (BuNo 126672). Given the pressing concerns of the war, development of the Cougar was given the highest priority. The XF9F-6 (BuNo 126670) first flew on 20 September 1951, with Grumman test pilot Fred Rowley at the controls and in line with Grumman's tradition of naming its fighter aircraft after felines, was named Cougar, as it represented a marked break from the Panther design.

Although featuring swept-wings and a swept horizontal tail surface, the Cougar shared many of the Panther's features, including a common engine, undercarriage, and core fuselage shape. The wings were swept-back at a 35-degree angle and the wing root and inlet fairing was positioned forward so as to properly position the center of lift for the swept-wing. The wingtip tanks, famous on the Panther, were obviously eliminated and 78 gallons of additional fuel was contained internally in each of the wings, for a total of 919 gallons. When the XF9F-6 was presented to the Navy for flight tests, it featured a combination of unboosted ailerons and wing spoilers, called flaperons, the latter a new feature. Slats were substituted for the leading-edge flaps, but the trailing-edge and fuselage flaps from the F9F-5 were retained and reshaped to the new wing design. A second speed brake was added via modified fuselage flaps.

The Cougar quickly experienced roll and pitch control problems that led to removal of the ailerons altogether. The spoilers were then extended inboard and outboard, and split into two sections, the aft section being hydraulically controlled via a second hydraulic system to serve as a backup. The aft sections were called flaperettes. A small aileron called the "wing trimmer" was retained on the left wing for roll-trim control. These modifications solved the roll control issues, but did not cure the pitch-up problem. That required yet another innovation, the installation of a large wing fence, plus the reshaping of the upper aft portion of the wing-to-fuse-lage fillet. Moreover, the leading edge of the wing just outboard of the engine intakes was rounded. One further modification involved the installation of what was called a "flying tail"—a hydraulically controlled horizontal stabilizer, which moved in tandem with the elevators. This provided critical pitch control at high-speed flight now possible with the Cougar's swept-wing design.

Flight testing at NATC began in February 1952 and carrier suitability tests were performed by aircraft 126257 and 126258 aboard USS Midway (CVB-41) in mid-August. By the year's end, the F9F-6 was assigned to fleet squadron with VF-32, which deployed aboard USS Tarawa (CV-40) in November 1953. VF-24, assigned to USS Yorktown (CV-10), was the first squadron to actually deploy with the Cougar (in August), but was too late arriving in theater to participate in the air war. Once in service, some F9F-6s were fitted with an AN/ARA-25 UHF homing antennae in an under-nose fairing.

## Cougar Performance

From a performance standpoint, the Cougar was vastly superior to the Panther. With an empty weight of 11,483 lbs, the F9F-6 had a maximum speed of Mach .79 (about 650 mph) at sea level and Mach .895 at 35,000 feet with a combat load (16,244 pounds). It had a 933-mile range, which could be extended with the use of two 150-gallon wing tanks. As noted earlier, the F9F-6 was initially powered by the same J42-P-6 used in the F9F-5 Panther. In fact, this engine was used in the first 30 production Cougars, but was then replaced by the 7,250-lbf J42-P-8. The engine in the XF9F-6 was also replaced with the P-8. A total of 646 F9F-6s were produced in a production run that commenced 28 December 1951 and ended on 2 July 1954.[cxx]

The F9F-6 was known as a highly maneuverable and easy-to-fly aircraft, and many pilots described it as handling "better behind the boat" than the F9F-5. Although the F9F-6

*The Cougar production line in full swing. Indicative of this transitional era in jet aircraft design, the first three F11F Tigers can be seen taking shape in a special line-up (at extreme left). The Tiger was Grumman's first operational supersonic aircraft, even though the transonic Cougars could occasionally exceed Mach 1 in a dive.* (Northrop Grumman History Center)

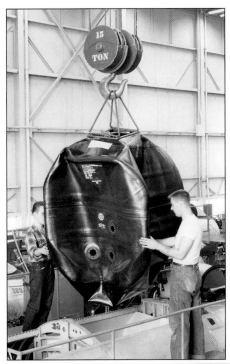

*A fuel bladder is installed in the center fuselage structure of an F9F-6 Cougar.* (Jim Sullivan Collection)

*Top front three-quarter view of the Cougar with the full wing fence installed. Despite the wing and horizontal tailplanes having been modified from straight to swept, notice that the Cougar's vertical stabilizer remained identical in shape with that of the Panther.* (Northrop Grumman History Center)

*An F9F-6 evaluates odd-looking, but very aerodynamically shaped fuel tanks during a test flight. Despite their aerodynamic efficiency, these tanks were never used operationally.* (Naval Aviation Museum)

just missed the Korean War, the Navy put it to good use and set a then-world-transcontinental-crossing record on 1 April 1954. Three pilots from VF-21 made the 2,438-mile flight in less than four hours, with LCdr. F. X. Brady recording the fastest time of 3 hours 45 minutes and 30 seconds. His aircraft, number 131047, reportedly averaged 648.69 mph during the flight. Lt. W. Rich and Lt. (j.g.) J. C. Barrow accompanied him. The three aircraft refueled

from an AJ Savage over Kansas using an experimental refueling probe mounted in the nose cone. An F9F-6 from VF-21 (BuNo 131062) was also one of the first jets to launch from a steam catapult in tests aboard USS *Hancock* (CVA-19). The F9F-6 served in fleet units until February 1956, when VF-142, which had returned from its cruise aboard USS *Boxer* (CV-21), transitioned to the newer F9F-8s. The F9F-6 served with 20 Navy fleet squadrons

*The Cougar prototype is seen here on its maiden flight.* (Northrop Grumman History Center)

*The Cougar's wing folded vertically to 90 degrees, much like the original XF9F-2 and XF9F-3 designs prior to the addition of the wingtip tanks. This Cougar belongs to VF-24 and is deployed aboard USS* Yorktown *(CV-10).* (Naval Aviation Museum)

The first F9F-7 appears on the Grumman tarmac in 1954. A total of 168 F9F-7s were ordered, but the final 50 were built as F9F-6s with the J48-P-8 turbojet engine. (Naval Aviation Museum)

An F9F-7 lands aboard USS Coral Sea (CV-43) during NATC carrier suitability tests. (Naval Aviation Museum)

An excellent view of a VF-24 F9F-6 with flaps lowered, tailhook extended but raised, and both upper fuselage air intakes open. (Jim Sullivan Collection)

F9F-7 (BuNo 130850) belonging to the Naval Air Reserve was photographed at Wichita, Kansas, in 1959. (Bill Larkins via Jim Sullivan Collection)

The upgraded F9F-6 Cougar cockpit retained the same basic layout as the previous Panther cockpits, but featured improved instrumentation and avionics over its predecessor. (Jim Sullivan Collection)

Left-hand cockpit console of the Cougar was nearly identical to the Panther to ease pilot training and transition from one airplane to the next. Placard at upper center reads: "For Max Windshield Defrosting Close Foot Canopy and Cabin Outlets." (Northrop Grumman Corporation)

but no active Marine Corps squadrons. As the newer Cougars entered the fleet, F9F-6s were assigned to at least 23 Navy Reserve and various Marine Corps Reserve Air Training Detachments.

## The F9F-7—Another Alternative Engine Design

As with the F9F-2 and F9F-5, an alternative engine version of the F9F-6 was produced as the F9F-7. The -7 featured the same 6,350-lbf Allison J33-A-16A found in the F9F-4. Of the 168 F9F-7s ordered, the final 50 were built with the J48-P-8. While one can understand Grumman's initial concerns during the late 1940s with the availability of a new engine design as well as the uncertainties surrounding a new-comer to the jet engine field, Pratt & Whitney, after what can only be described as failures with the -3 and -4 alternative designs, it seems surprising that Grumman would repeat this mistake a third time. The F9F-7 made only one carrier deployment and served only in VFs-21 and -61 for a short period of time between mid-1953 and early 1954, and was otherwise assigned to Reserve units. Moreover, as with the -3 and -4, most of the F9F-7s were re-engined with the J48-P-8.

## The F9F-7 Flexible Deck Experiment

One of the more interesting concepts experimented with during the 1950s was the British-inspired flexible deck. The theory behind the design was simple enough—if landing gear, which comprised some 33 percent of the aircraft's weight—could be eliminated, the aircraft would gain greater range and could carry more ordnance. Moreover, if each aircraft weighed less, more could be deployed on an aircraft carrier, thereby increasing its offensive potential. The Royal Navy had been experimenting with the so-called flex deck concept since the late 1940s using a modified de Havilland Vampire. The United States Navy and Air Force, which got wind of these developments, were extremely interested and

The British conducted flexible deck experiments in the late-1940s using the de Havilland Vampire. Two Grumman test pilots who visited Farnborough to observe the Royal Navy tests in person were both permitted to fly the Vampire using the flex deck system. (Tommy Thomason)

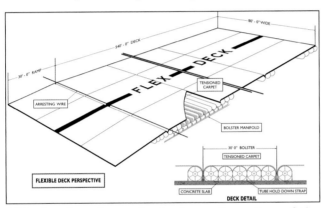

This drawing shows the basic configuration of the landing area used for the flex-deck tests. Dimensions are 30 feet for the ramp at left, 540 feet for the landing area, and 80 feet wide. Bolsters of "tensioned carpet" are arranged in 30-foot sections on a concrete slab. (Northrop Grumman History Center, redrawn by Matt Sheppard)

Two F9F-7 Cougars were modified for similar U.S. Navy flex deck tests. Shown here is BuNo 130862. The boxed undercarriage can clearly be seen in this image. The white stripes and hash marks are for photo calibration of the upcoming tests. (Northrop Grumman History Center)

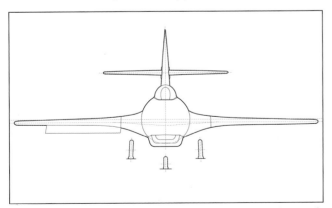

This front-view of the flex-deck F9F-7 reveals modifications made to the underside of the fuselage as well as the increased wing flap area. One can only imagine the penalty paid in induced drag. (Northrop Grumman History Center, redrawn by Matt Sheppard)

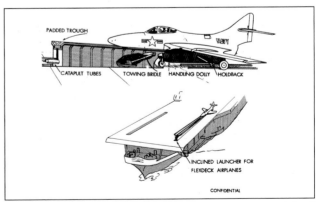

This illustration depicts how the flex-deck modified Cougar would have been launched from the aircraft carrier. The launch method envisioned an inclined ramp and utilized a handling dolly to serve as temporary landing gear. (Northrop Grumman History Center)

*An F9F-7 makes an arrested landing on the rubber flex deck surface during the 1955 NATC tests. All tests were conducted on land. While tests proved that landing was certainly possible, the problem came in how to quickly and efficiently move the aircraft about the deck once they were recovered.* (Northrop Grumman History Center)

contracted to design and test such a system. Grumman was asked to provide two modified F9F-7 aircraft for the tests, which were redesignated as Design 94A. The two aircraft, BuNos. 130862 and 130863, were fitted with a 3-inch-deep false bottom under the center fuselage to balance the airframe and were given the more powerful J48-P-8 turbojet engine. Portions of the leading-edge slats were bolted in the down position and the center flaps were locked in the shut position to prevent damage from contact with the deck surface.

In September, two of the Grumman project test pilots, Russ Schwarting and Norm Coutant, and various Navy personnel visited Farnborough, England, to observe first hand how the British were using the system, and each made repeated landings in the Vampire. Upon their return, one of the Grumman test pilots, Norm Coutant, who had made eight landings in the Vampire, commented that the system seemed impractical as it involved too much pilot skill, especially if it was to be used at sea.

The U.S. Navy project began in February 1955 at the NATC at Patuxent River, Maryland. A flexible deck measuring 375 feet long and 80 feet wide (the size of the landing area on a carrier) was constructed of rubberized fabric carpet lubricated with oil and water. The rubber mat made by Goodyear measured 1/2-inch thick. A series of arresting cables were installed on the deck. On 18 February one of the modified F9F-7s made the program's first arrested landing. Grumman test pilot John Norris made at least 10 landings at 135 mph, which was used to ensure a safe fly-out in the event of a wire or hook failure. NATC test pilots Lt. John Moore and Maj. Ralph Feliton made another 13, and reported that the system worked well.

Aircraft weight was kept approximately the same for all flights and all were made with the same level approach. Only the height at which the wire/hook engagement was made was changed so that an evaluation could be made of the best heights for various loads. According to an internal Grumman report:

*Right-hand cockpit console of the Cougar retained same basic layout for the radios and nav gear, but knobs and dials were slightly larger and easier to manipulate than earlier designs in the Panther. Circuit-breaker panel was also in same location.* (Northrop Grumman Corporation)

In-flight refueling helped the VF-21 Cougars make their cross-country flight. This North American AJ-2 Savage refueled the Cougars using the Navy's now-standard hose-and-drogue system somewhere over Oklahoma. (Northrop Grumman History Center)

Four Cougars are parked Tail Over Water (TOW) along the edge of the carrier deck. Although the type had a two-year jump on other swept-wing fighters, the F9F-6 did not remain in fleet squadron operation for very long. The North American FJ-3 Fury replaced the early model Cougar and Grumman's own more advanced F9F-8/8B. (Jim Sullivan Collection)

VF-112 had a long history in the F9F, transitioning to the F9F-2 in 1950 and then to the F9F-5 in 1953, before moving into the Cougar later that year. The squadron made one deployment with the F9F-6 aboard USS Kearsarge (CV-33) from 7 October 1954 through 12 May 1955, then upgraded to the F9F-8 in June 1956. (Jim Sullivan Collection)

A VF-113 F9F-8 Cougar is seconds from launch off USS Essex (CV 9). The bridle attachment used for launch is clearly apparent. (National Archives)

Two F9F-6 Cougars from VF-24 are ready to launch from USS Yorktown (CV-10) in October 1953. (Bert Kinzy, Detail & Scale, Inc.)

*A pilot wearing full flight and survival gear stands ready to enter the cockpit of his F9F-6 Cougar aboard the USS* Randolph *(CV-15).* (Northrop Grumman History Center)

The U.S. flex deck program continued flight tests until August 1955 and was finally terminated in March 1956. Overall, the results were deemed a success. However, the true benefit of the demonstration, reducing aircraft weight by removing landing gear, could not be realized, as that meant that any aircraft that needed to divert to a land base had no means to land. There were also concerns about how the aircraft, which had no undercarriage, would be moved about the carrier flight deck and still provide a reasonable landing schedule for other aircraft. It was feared that it would take too long to re-spot the aircraft and thus, would ultimately hamper flight operations.

### The F9F-6 at the Boat

"The first of the 10 landings was made at an engagement height of 11 inches, the second and third at 15, the fourth at 24, and the height was increased gradually until it reached 44 to 46 inches. (After this one, John commented that he didn't know why anyone would want to come in way up there.) As the heights increased, the pilot felt the loads more but the protective device functioned well and the pilot reported the discomfort to be minor, and recommended the system. Incidentally, witnesses and the people who studied the films of the landings were amazed at John Norris' consistent ability to put the airplane into the grove, exactly as required."[cxxi]

Given the concerns about the decreased lift associated with swept-wing designs, modifications had to be made to the Cougar's carrier landing approach to ensure safe handling. Generally speaking, for carrier landings with no external stores, the F9F-6 Flight Manual recommended an approach speed of 120 knots (± 2 knots). Engine RPMs required by the approach varied depending on the gross weight of the recovering aircraft from approximately 85 percent RPM at 15,550 pounds to 80 percent RPM at 13,500 pounds. It was recommended that pilots add an additional 2 percent RPM in the steepest part of the approach's turn to avoid decelerating, but then reduce power the same amount on rolling out "in the groove" to avoid accelerating.

*An VF-112 F9F-8B (BuNo. 141066) "bolters" (misses all the arresting cables after touching down on the deck) while landing aboard an unnamed angle-deck aircraft carrier.* (Jim Sullivan Collection)

VC-61 transitioned from its F9F-5Ps to the swept-wing F9F-6P. The Cougar was faster and handled better than the straight-wing variant and was welcomed by Navy pilots. After serving in fleet units, the F9F-6P was relegated to Reserve squadrons. (Jim Sullivan Collection)

A look at the F9F-6P cockpit shows the cameras' viewfinder for aerial photography located in the center of the instrument panel. (Northrop Grumman History Center)

*During flight tests, a Cougar (BuNo 126670) shed part of its tail. However, the aircraft continued to handle well, which gave test pilots the desire to see whether such a design could indeed work. The shorter tail section reduced drag, which would enhance combat performance, but Grumman engineers and aerodynamicists questioned the tradeoff in less lateral stability. In two test flights, numbers 209 and 210, the "short vertical tail" was evaluated in approach profiles, but ultimately proved too difficult to control.* (Jim Sullivan Collection)

Since the approach "in the groove"—the time period where the approaching plane is immediately behind the carrier—is usually no longer than 5 to 10 seconds, major corrections in airspeed and altitude had to be made before getting into the groove. The Cougar, with its swept-wing design, possessed a somewhat higher angle-of-attack versus the straight-wing Panthers, and for this reason, the induced drag was considerably higher, which meant that even slight reductions in thrust resulted in a rather rapid deceleration. Moreover, noticeably larger increases in thrust were needed to increase the aircraft's speed, especially when correcting a low or slow landing approach. In short, the manual was clear—a pilot was not to take off too much power when in the groove. Equally so, after reaching the cut, the Cougar pilot was to establish and maintain a steady descent and cautioned not to flare the aircraft.

Waive-offs were also a bit trickier with the Cougar. As the Flight Manual stated, "[a] swept-wing airplane is a little slower to accelerate on a waive-off than a straight-wing airplane, because the drag, in the landing configuration, is greater for the swept wing."[cxxii] Given that fact, Cougar pilots were cautioned not to wait too long to take a waive-off. Likewise, because a jet engine responds slower than a reciprocating engine, it was necessary to maintain at least 65-percent RPM while making final approach, in order to ensure a rapid waive-off. For

waive-offs, pilots were instructed to immediately push full throttle, raise landing gear once clear of the deck, and to raise flaps once airspeed rose above 150 knots. Fuel conservation and awareness was also important, as approximately 220 pounds of fuel were needed to go around and resume the landing pattern.

## In-Flight Refueling

Some of the F9F-6 Cougars were equipped for in-flight refueling of the two main tanks. Refueling was accomplished by means of a system consisting of a probe, additional piping and valves, and further venting in the main fuel cells. Fuel flow was regulated largely by control of the tanker aircraft's pump pressure and typically amounted to 1,200 pounds per minute on the tanker pressure pump and 300 pounds per minute on the low-pressure or emergency pump. Refueling was accomplished from aircraft fitted with a tanking kit, consisting of a fuel cell, a high-pressure pump, a low-pressure or emergency pump, a reel with 70 feet of hose on the end of which was affixed a drogue. Only the two fuselage tanks could be refueled. Thus, it was recommended that where refueling was planned, pilots first use the fuselage fuel, and reserve the wing tanks for later use.

Cougars used the ARA-25 homing equipment or ARN-6 radio compass to rendezvous with the tanker.

Both systems would be tuned to the tanker's equipment. The F9F-6 Flight Manual described the process as follows:

"After rendezvous has been affected, close in on the tanker from astern until flying in steady state with the probe approximately 10 feet aft and below the tanker drogue. This will place the airplane clear of the tanker's prop wash. The highest speed the tanker can maintain with the drogue extended will allow the most comfortable attitude for the receiver airplane. With present configurations, this speed is approximately 200 knots IAS. This is approximately the speed of the F9F-6 at which the RPM required is at a minimum. If lower speeds are desired, power must be added. Observe the lights on the tanker, an amber light indicating that the tanker is ready to deliver fuel. Set the in-flight refueling switch to FUEL. Shift to 100 percent oxygen. Add 4 to 5 percent RPM and allow the fighter to accelerate slowly, but steadily, flying the probe into the funnel surrounding the drogue."[cxxiii]

Cougar pilots were to watch the fuel quantity gauge and when it showed the tanks to be within 400 pounds of full, they were to notify the tanker by radio to shift to emergency pump, which would then shut off when the tanks were full. To detach from the tanker, the pilot reduced his RPM 4 to 5 percent and then allowed a steady rate of opening away from the tanker to develop until it was clear to withdraw.

## The F9F-6P Photo Cougar

As with the two primary versions of the Panther, a photoreconnaissance version of the Cougar was also produced. Virtually identical to the F9F-6, the -6P was about 250 pounds lighter and utilized the same camera configurations, as did the F9F-5. The production run, which lasted from 19 June 1954 through 25 March 1955, produced 60 F9F-6Ps. Ironically, production of this variant ended just two months prior to the beginning of production of the F9F-8P discussed later. Production aircraft included BuNos 127473 through 127492, 128295 through 128310, 131252 through 131255, and 134446 through 123465. The Cougar marked the Navy's first swept-wing photoreconnaissance aircraft and served with three reconnaissance squadrons.

## Drone Variants

As with Panthers, as the F9F-6s were removed from service, many found their way into service as drone and drone director aircraft. The drones were designated as the F9F-6K (later, QDF-9F) and the drone controller aircraft was designated as the F9F-6D (later the D9F-6F). Another designation, dubbed F9F-6K2 (QF-9G), represented F9F-6Ks equipped with modernized equipment, hence, an improved drone configuration.

*Shown here is F9F-6 (BuNo 131047), one of the VF-21 Cougars that set the transcontinental speed record on 9 April 1956, flying the route from San Diego to New York in only 3 hours and 45 minutes. Maximum airspeed achieved on that flight was 665 mph.* (Bill Larkins via Jim Sullivan Collection)

An NATC pilot takes off during carrier suitability tests flying BuNo 131067. Notice the "FT" for "Flight Test" on the nose above the aircraft number. Catapult bridle can be seen on the carrier's deck directly under the aircraft's tail section. (Jim Sullivan Collection)

Combat-ready swept-wing F9F-8 Cougar rides the deck-edge elevator from the carrier's hangar deck up to the flight deck. This aircraft belongs to Navy Fighter Squadron VF-121 and wears very distinctive red accent markings on nose, tail, and wingtips. (Tommy Thomason)

# CHAPTER EIGHT

# THE ULTIMATE COUGAR

*VF-61's Jolly Rogers transitioned to the F9F-7 Cougar in August 1953 from the F9F-5, and then replaced its -7s with F9F-6 Cougars in May 1954. The squadron deployed aboard USS Lake Champlain (CV-39) then traded its Cougars for North American FJ-3 Furies. The squadron then transitioned to the F9F-8 in January 1956, with which it deployed aboard USS Intrepid (CV-11). Following that deployment, the Cougars were replaced by F3H-2M Demons. The operations here are aboard Intrepid.* (Naval Aviation Museum)

Although the F9F-6 Cougar offered many performance advancements over the Panther, the ultimate Cougar came in the F9F-8 and the F9F-8B, which first appeared in 1954. Indeed, if any of the Cougar's limitations must at all be called shortcomings, they can be largely attributed to the fact that the jet was rushed through design and flight tests in order to have a deployable swept-wing Navy fighter for the Korean War to match the MiG-15. Even as the F9F-6 was being flown by Grumman and NATC test pilots, Grumman engineers were already at work on an improved version of the Cougar, which would become the definitive design.

## The F9F-8 Cougar

Work on Design 99, which became the F9F-8 Cougar, began in April 1953 with three goals: (1) to reduce the Cougar's stall speed; (2) to improve aircraft control at high angles of attack; and (3) to increase the Cougar's range. The changes were largely in the fuselage and wing, with the former including an 8-inch extension of the center fuselage. The first two goals were accomplished by replacing the slats outboard of the wing fences with extended and cambered leading edges, which created a snag or a "dog-tooth." The trailing edges were also extended aft. Wing chord was modified to 15 percent, which increased total wing area from 300 to 337 square feet and also resulted in a relatively thinner wing section, which had the added benefit of slightly increasing the F9F-8's top speed. Together, these modifications helped enhance the overall performance behind the boat. Adding a 30-gallon fuel tank in the leading edge of each wing and enlarging the forward fuel tank extended the Cougar's range. Total fuel for the F9F-8 was 1,068 gallons, an increase of 149 gallons.

The F9F-8 was powered by the same 7,250-lbf J48-P-8A turbojet. Other improvements included a fixed in-flight refueling probe on the nose and a reinforced sliding canopy. Also, in contrast to the split location of the ammunition boxes of most Panthers and the F9F-6, all four ammunition boxes were mounted above the guns. As with earlier Panthers and F9F-6 Cougars, many of the F9F-8s were later fitted with the UHF homing antennae in an under-nose fairing. Wiring and controls for use of the AIM-9 Sidewinder were also added to late-production Cougars and retrofitted into earlier models. Another modification that arose later in production was the addition of a boundary layer splitter plate between the intake and fuselage. Early production F9F-8s simply had fuselage skin as the inner wall on the intake.

A total of 601 F9F-8s were built between 29 April 1954 and 22 March 1957. The F9F-8s first flight took place on 18 January 1954, with Corky Meyer at the controls. Navy Board of Inspection and Survey (BIS) Trials began on 17 December 1954 and were followed by land-based suitability tests at NATC. A total of 96 catapult launches were made, with 117 arresting gear recoveries.

Three at-sea carrier acceptance periods, one running from 24 January to 1 February 1955 aboard USS *Coral Sea* (CVB-43), and the second running from 27 April through 6 May aboard USS *Bennington* (CV-20) followed.[cxxiv] A third carrier suitability test was conducted in September, lasting from the 12th through the 16th aboard USS *Ticonderoga* (CVA-14), which was fitted with the C11-1 steam catapult and the Mk 7 Mod 1-1 double-reeved, constant-pressure arresting gear. Seven catapult launches were made to establish minimum catapult end air speeds, and six arrested landings were made to determine loads imposed on the aircraft and the operational limitations under shipboard conditions. Per the tests, the lowest catapult speed was 127 knots (a combined

**This overhead view of the F9F-8 shows the increased wing area versus the F9F-6 and -7, and highlights the changes made to the flaps and ailerons. Note the new "sawtooth" leading edge created by the chord extension outboard of the wing fences.** (Jim Sullivan Collection)

**In this view, the same Cougar presents a beautiful silhouette. Wing fences can be easily seen as well as the flaps, highlighted in white.** (Northrop Grumman History Center)

figure of catapult end-speed and wind-over-deck). The minimums were governed by sink off the bow and entry into airframe buffet. Approximately 25 feet of sink off the bow occurred at the noted 127-knot speed. The YF9F-8 prototype, aircraft 131067, was used for the three at-sea periods, as was 131227 while at NATC. In all, 58 catapult launches and 54 arrested landings were completed during the three periods.

Armament tests took place in late 1954 and early 1955 using aircraft 131073. A total of 80 flights and 111 flight hours were conducted, resulting in minor changes to the guns. Overall, the armament system was accepted into service, although the Mk 3's firing performance under zero and negative g-forces was deemed unsatisfactory. Other problems encountered included breakage of the gun trigger solenoid, link jams, and insufficient gun gas elimination. The report concluded that the guns tracking capabilities of the F9F-8 were "greatly improved over those exhibited by the Model F9F-6 airplane."[cxxv]

The F9F-8 Cougar had a top speed of 714 mph and a range of 1,000 miles without drop tanks. Although clearly a subsonic design, the new Cougar could break the sound barrier in steep dives. Cruising speed for the F9F-8 was approximately 516 mph and landing speed was set at 132 mph. It had a service ceiling of 42,000 feet and could climb to an altitude of 20,000 feet in 4 minutes. On internal tanks, the F9F-8 had a range of 1,050 miles. With two 150-gallon tanks, this could be extended to 1,363 miles.

VF-13 based at NAS Cecil Field, Florida, was the first Navy squadron to receive the F9F-8, while VF-121 was the first F9F-8 equipped squadron to deploy. VF-121 took the Cougar to sea in mid-1955 aboard USS *Hancock* (CVA-19) for a WestPac cruise. More than 33 fleet squadrons eventually flew the F9F-8/8B, including both VF and VA squadrons, and the type made 16 carrier deployments.[cxxvi] The F9F-8 has been heralded as the

*Another production line image finds two-seat F9F-8T Cougars being built alongside of two different versions of the S-2A Tracker, one an anti-submarine patrol plane in foreground, and a twin-tail E-1B Tracer about to be fitted with a large radar dish antenna atop the fuselage.* (Northrop Grumman History Center)

*This aft view looking forward shows a good presentation of the flaps in their lowest position. Large twin-engine amphibian at right is a Coast Guard Grumman SA-16 Albatross air-sea rescue aircraft.* (Jim Sullivan Collection)

*The Bethpage production line shows a bevy of tail sections for the F9F-8 in various stages of completion.* (Northrop Grumman History Center)

*The air intake at the wing root was refashioned by adding a boundary layer splitter plate, seen here in this image of BuNo 141668. On prior versions this area was simply the contoured fuselage itself.* (Jim Sullivan Collection)

*The Marine Corps used the two-seat Cougar for training, as with VMT-2, shown here, and in its H&MS squadrons.* (Naval Aviation Museum)

and added a tailhook. The Sabre's six .50-cal guns were replaced with the Navy's required 20mm cannon and a wing fold mechanism was installed. The first of three XFJ-2 prototypes flew in February 1952 and sea trials were conducted in December aboard USS *Coral Sea* (CVA-43). Because of the added weight associated with the modifications to accommodate carrier use, the XFJ-2 proved underpowered. As a result, the Navy cut back production of the FJ-2 and ordered the FJ-3, which featured the Wright J65 engine, rated at 7,800 lbf. The FJ-3 reached the fleet in 1955, two years after the Cougar. Although the FJ-3s fleet service was plagued by a series of engine problems, it served longer in the fleet fighter role than the Cougar. Author Tommy Thomason attributes this more to the fact that the Cougar had an attack role that was being superseded by new jets, such as the Douglas A4D-1 Skyhawk, rather than due to any deficiency in the F9F-6/-8 itself. Thomason explained:

"The reason that the FJ-3 was deployed longer and a little more often (19 times vs. 16) in fighter squadrons than the F9F-8 probably wasn't because it was the better fighter. More likely it was because it had a minimal capability as an attack aircraft, whereas the F9F-8 was good for that too, including nuclear weapon delivery. In effect, the F9F-8 was a jet attack placeholder along with the F7U-3M, while the pipeline was being filled with FJ-4Bs and A4Ds. As a result, the FJ-3 was the designated day fighter by default on most deployments."[cxxix]

This observation also seems backed up by comments from Corky Meyer, who flew both the Cougar and FJ-3 Fury. Meyer noted that the Cougar had greater endurance, possessed a higher dive speed limit, and was more maneuverable.

"[The] Combat Air Patrol mission was for two hours on station at 150 nm from the carrier. This required 2+30 takeoff, cruise, and landing endurance plus reserves. The F9F-6 could perform a three-hour CAP mission on internal fuel. The FJ-2 and -3 with external tanks had less than 1+30 mission time and the FJ-4 just met the mission requirement."

to Argentina to support training of its Panther crews. These were assigned serials 0516 and 0517 and based at NAN Comandante Espora. They were withdrawn from service in 1971.

## Other Swept-Wing Fighters of the Day

The F9F-6 Cougar was the Navy's sole swept-wing fighter for approximately two years. Although it was too late to participate in the Korean War, it nevertheless served the Navy well and was regarded as the best swept-wing fighter of its time. Perhaps its most visible competitor was the swept-wing version of the North American FJ Fury, designated as the FJ-2, and later the FJ-3. The FJ-2 program was an effort to bring to the Navy the successful design of the F-86 Sabre, which the Air Force had developed in the late 1940s and deployed with much success over the skies of North Korea against the MiG-15.

To accommodate the vigorous nature of carrier operations, North American redesigned the Sabre's landing gear to accommodate the added stress of carrier landings

The only version of the Cougar to see combat was the F9F-8T used by H&MS-13 during the early years of the Vietnam War. (National Museum of Naval Aviation)

Moreover, the FJ-3 had a dive limit of Mach 1 and a 6-g maneuvering limit, while the Cougar could dive at Mach 1.2 and had a 7.5-g maneuvering limit.

### F9F-9: An Outgrowth of the Panther/Cougar

An offshoot of the Panther/Cougar program began in late 1952 by Grumman designer Joseph Gavin with the goal of producing a supersonic fighter using the F9F Panther as the starting point. Hoping to recreate its success transitioning the Panther into a successful swept-wing fighter, Grumman began work on Design 98, using the core Panther and incorporating the NACA-developed "Area Rule" concept to reduce transonic drag. The area

Some squadrons, such as VF-111, shown here, retained a two-seat Cougar for proficiency training. Note Korean War–era Douglas AD Skyraider in background at left. (Jim Sullivan Collection)

It must have been pretty cold in the cockpit that day as this F9F-8T conducts open-cockpit testing near Grumman's new, large Calverton facility on the eastern end of Long Island, about 60 miles east of Bethpage. Careful observation reveals an earlier-style rear windshield ahead of the rear cockpit. Note fully enclosed helmets being worn by both crewmen. Shadow on aircraft's nose is being cast by the photo aircraft. (Jim Sullivan Collection)

*This line of two-seat Cougars highlights the second windscreen for the aft cockpit, allowing the aircraft to be flown with the canopy opened.* (Naval Aviation Museum)

rule (or transonic area rule) is an aircraft design technique used to reduce drag at transonic and supersonic speeds, especially between Mach 0.8 and 1.2. At high-subsonic flight speeds, supersonic airflow can develop in areas where the flow accelerates around the aircraft body and wings. The speed at which this occurs, known as the critical Mach number, varies from aircraft to aircraft. The resulting shock waves formed at these points of supersonic flow can bleed away a considerable amount of power, which the pilot experiences as a sudden and very powerful form of drag, called wave drag. To reduce the number and power of these shock waves, an aerodynamic shape should change in cross sectional area as smoothly as possible. This produces a "perfect" aerodynamic shape known as the Sears-Haack body—essentially a flattened, elongated ellipse.

According to the area rule, an aircraft designed with the same lengthwise cross-sectional area distribution as the Sears-Haack body generates the same wave drag regardless of its actual shape. Aircraft are therefore arranged so that large volume items such as wings are positioned at the widest area of the equivalent Sears-Haack body, and that the cockpit, tailplane, intakes, and other "bulges" are spread out along the fuselage so that the rest of the fuselage along these "bulges" is correspondingly thinned. In plan view, the fuselage can be described as "wasp-waist" in shape, similar to that of a Coke bottle. Hence, the popular name applied to the body of an area-rule aircraft was "Coke bottle fuselage."

The new aircraft was at the time dubbed the XF9F-8. Grumman almost immediately realized that the modifications would take the design well beyond its original intentions. Thus, by the spring of 1953, Design 98 had morphed into an entirely new aircraft with little in common with the Panther or Cougar. A new study then began on limited modifications of the F9F-6, which would become Design 99 and would result in the F9F-8.

A contract was issued on 27 April 1953 calling for three XF9F-9 aircraft, despite the fact that the aircraft was no longer a derivative of the F9F. After instrumented model tests using a small replica of the design mounted on the nose boom of an F9F-6, a supplemental contract was issued calling for production of 42 additional F9F-9s. The F11F-1 Tiger first flew on 30 July 1954 and went on to be the first Navy fighter to reach Mach 1. The F11F-1F Super Tiger, which was the first to break Mach 2 (in 1958), was never placed in production. The Tiger had a limited, four-year service career, being replaced by the larger and more powerful Vought F-8 Crusader. The F9F-9 designation continued in use until April 1955, when the aircraft was redesignated as the F11F-1.

# CHAPTER NINE

# BLUE ANGELS AND PANTHERS IN FOREIGN SERVICE

*Anyone lucky enough to have seen the Blue Angels flying their new F9F-8 Cougars back in the 1950s witnessed a rare treat. This model boxtop depicts an imaginary formation racing past the grandstands at a Naval Air Station somewhere in the Eastern U.S. Note the team's support C-54 Skymaster parked in the background.* (Mike Machat for Revell of Mexico.)

*Four F9F-6 Blue Angels are parked nose to nose, with their respective plots waving from the cockpits. Respecting the Navy/Marine tradition, a Marine pilot flies the Number Two aircraft.* (Northrop Grumman History Center)

*Although at first glance appearing to be a single airplane, these are actually four Blue Angels' Cougars in tight formation. In certain show maneuvers, wingtip-to-canopy separation between team aircraft was as close as 36 inches.* (Northrop Grumman History Center)

A formation of F9F-8 Blue Angels is seen over the beaches of Pensacola, Florida, diving down to "Show Center" while practicing for an upcoming air show. Team schedule during show season includes two practice shows per day during the week preceding an actual public appearance. (Northrop Grumman History Center)

*The 1958 Blue Angels team members pose by the tail of one of the Blue Angels' Cougars.* (Northrop Grumman History Center)

Revised markings on the second Blue Angels' F9F-8T (BuNo 147404) show the new tail number "7," plus yellow vertical fin cap. Blue Angels script logotype and new shield adorn the airplane's forward fuselage, while the "U.S. Navy" titles have been relocated to the upper aft fuselage. Note the in-flight refueling probe painted yellow on the aircraft's nose. (Bert Kinzey)

The Blue Angels used a two-seat F9F-8T (BuNo 142470) for VIP, media, and training flights. Notice the "0" on the tail rather than the typical number "1" through "6." This aircraft's tail number was later changed to the number "7," and the team's two-seater has remained as "Blue Angels Number Seven" to this day. The two-seat Cougar was replaced by the McDonnell F-4D Phantom II, the Douglas TA-4J Skyhawk, and the McDonnell Douglas F/A-18 Hornet still being flown by the team today. (Northrop Grumman History Center)

A ground-crew member works on one of the Panthers, No. 118. This aircraft was U.S. BuNo 127099 and is now on display at the Argentine Naval Museum. (Steve Ginter)

A division of F9F-2s flies over Argentina. The Panthers were not able to launch from the sole Argentinean carrier because its catapult was not powerful enough. (Steve Ginter)

This poor-quality photo is one of the extremely rare images that shows all of the Panthers purchased by the Argentinean Navy. The F9F-2s served with the squadron until 1971. (Steve Ginter)

# F9F SERVICE DESIGNATIONS

| Pre-1962 | Unified System Post-September 1962 | Pre-1962 | Unified System Post-September 1962 |
|----------|-----------------------------------|----------|-----------------------------------|
| F9F-5D | DF-9E | F9F-7 | F-9H |
| F9F-5P | N/A | F9F-8 | F-9J, QF-9J |
| F9F-6 | F-9F | F9F-8B | YAF-9J, QF-9J |
| F9F-6D | DF-9F | F9F-8P | RF-9J |
| F9F-6K | QF-9F, QF-9G | F9F-8T | YTF-9J, TF-9J |

# U.S. NAVY/MARINE CORPS PANTHER/COUGAR SQUARDONS

## U.S. NAVY

| Squadron | Nickname | Types Flown | Squadron | Nickname | Types Flown |
|----------|----------|-------------|----------|----------|-------------|
| VF-13 | Aggressors | F9F-6/8/8T | VF-74 | Bedevilers | F9F-6 |
| VF-21 | Mach Busters | F9F-2/5/7 | VF-76/VA-76 | Spirits | F9F-8/8B |
| VF-23/VA-23 | Flashers | F9F-2/5/8/8B | VF-81 | Waldomen | F9F-5/6 |
| VF-24 | Corsairs | F9F-2/6 | VF-82 | Ironmen | F9F-5 |
| VA-26 | unknown | F9F-2 | VF-91 | Red Lightnings | F9F-2/6 |
| VF-31 | Tomcatters | F9F-2 | VF-92 | Silver Kings | F9F-2/5 |
| VF-32 | Fighting Swordsmen | F9F-6 | VF-93/VA-93 | Blue Blazers | F9F-2/5/8 |
| VF-33 | Tarsiers | F9F-6 | VF-94 | Tough Kitty | F9F-5/8 |
| VF-34/VA-34 | Blue Blasters | F9F-2 | VF-102/VA-36 | Roadrunners | F9F-5 |
| VA-36 | Road Runners | F9F-5/8/8B/8T | VF-103 | Sluggers | F9F-6 |
| VF-43 | Falcons | F9F-5/6/8 | VA-106 | Gladiators | F9F-8B |
| VA-44 | Hornets | F9F-8/8T | VF-111 | Sundowners | F9F-2/5/8/8B |
| VF-45 | Black Birds | F9F-8T | VF-112/ | | |
| VA-46 | Clansmen | F9F-5/8 | VA-112 | Custoda Pacis Armis | F9F-2B/3/5/6/8/8B |
| VF-51 | Screaming Eagles | F9F-2/3/2B/6 | VF-113 | Stingers | F9F-5/8 |
| VF-52 | Sealancers | F9F-2/2B/5/8/8B | VF-114 | Executioners | F9F-5 |
| VF-53 | Blue Knights | F9F-5/8 | VF-122 | Black Angels | F9F-8 |
| VA-54 | Hell's Angels | F9F-8B | VF-123 | Blue Racers/Haley's Comets | |
| VA-56 | Boomerangs | F9F-3/8/8B | | | F9F-2/8 |
| VF-61 | Jolly Rogers | F9F-2/6 | VF-124 | Moonlighters | F9F-2 |
| VF-63 | Fighting Red Cocks | F9F-5/6 | VA-125 | | |
| VF-64 | Freelancers | F9F-5 | (VA-26) | | F9F-8/8B |
| VA-66 | Waldos | F9F-5/8B | VA-126 | Bandits/Fighting Seahawks | F9F-8/8T |
| VF-71 | Fickle Finger Devils | F9F-2/5 | | | |
| VF-72/VA-72 | Hawks | F9F-2/5 | VF-142 | Fighting Falcons | F9F-6 |
| VF-73 | Tigers | F9F-5 | VF-143 | Cougars | F9F-6 |

| Squadron | Nickname | Types Flown |
|---|---|---|
| VF-144 | Bitterbirds | F9F-5/8B |
| VA-146 | Blacktails | F9F-8/8B |
| VF-151 | Black Knights | F9F-8 |
| VF-153 | Blue Tails Flies | F9F-2/5/6/8/8B |
| VA-156 | Iron Tigers | F9F-6/8B |
| VF-173 | Jesters | F9F-5/6 |
| VF-174/ | | |
| VA-176 | Hellrazors | F9F-6/8/8T |
| VF-191 | Satan's Kittens | F9F-2/2B/6 |
| VF-192/ | | |
| VA-192 | Golden Dragons/ | F9F-2/5/6/8B |
| | Goofy Loopes | |
| VA-212 | Rampant Raiders | F9F-8B |
| VA-214 | Volunteers | F9F-8/8B |
| VF-653 | | |
| (VF-151) | Dragons/ | F9F-2/5 |
| | Black Knights | |
| VF-671 | | |
| (VF-81) | Waldomen | F9F-5 |
| VF-721 | | |
| (VF-141) | Starbusters/ | F9F-2 |
| | Iron Angels | |
| VF-742 | | |
| (VF-82) | Iron Men | F9F-5 |
| VF-781 | | |
| (VF-121) | Peacemakers | F9F-2/5/6 |
| VF-783 | | |
| (VF-122) | Minute Men/ | F9F-2/5 |
| | Black Angels | |
| VF-791 | | |
| (VF-142) | Hammering Hosses/ | F9F-2/5/6 |
| | Fighting Falcons | |
| VF-821 | | |
| (VF-143) | Kingpins | F9F-2/6 |
| VF-831 | | |
| (VF-153) | Blue Tail Flies | F9F-2/5/6 |
| VF-837 | | |
| (VF-154) | Grand Slammers/ | F9F-2/5 |
| | Black Knights | |
| VF-916 | | |
| (VF-83) | Roaring Bulls | F9F-5 |
| VF-921 | | |
| (VF-84) | Cardinals/Bulls | F9F-5 |

## USMC

| Squadron | Nickname | Types Flown |
|---|---|---|
| VMF-114 | Death Dealers | F9F-8 |
| VMF-115 | Able Eagles | F9F-2/2B/4/5 |
| VMF-121 | Green Knights | F9F-8B |
| VMF-122 | Werewolves | F9F-4/5 |
| VMF-213 | Hell Hawks | F9F-4/5 |
| VMF-214 | Black Sheep | F9F-2/5 |
| VMF-223 | Bulldogs | F9F-2/4 |

| Squadron | Nickname | Types Flown |
|---|---|---|
| VMF-224 | Bengals | F9F-5 |
| VMF-232 | Red Devils | F9F-2 |
| VMF-234 | unknown | F9F-4 |
| VMF-235 | Death Angels | F9F-2 |
| VMF-311 | Willy Lovers | F9F-2/2B/5 |
| VMF-312 | Checkerboards | F9F-4 |
| VMF-314 | Black Knights | F9F-4/5 |
| VMF-323 | Death Rattlers | F9F-2/8 |
| VMF-334 | Falcons | F9F-4 |
| VMF-451 | Fighting Phillies | F9F-2 |
| VMA-533 | Night Hawks | F9F-8 |

## PHOTORECONNAISSANCE

| Squadron | | Types Flown |
|---|---|---|
| VC-61 | | F9F-2P/5P/6P |
| VC-62 | | F9F-8P |
| VCP-63 | | F9F-8P |
| VFP-61 | | F9F-8P/8T |
| VFP-62 | | F9F-8P/8T |
| VMJ/VMCJ-3 | | F9F-5P/8P |

## TRAINING COMMAND

### Air Training Units

During the 1950s, the Navy training structure was anything but straightforward. Type training was conducted by Air Training Units (ATUs), which helped transition students into jet aircraft. The Air Training Units included ATU-102/-202 at NAS Kingsville, Texas; ATU-201 at NAS Corpus Christi; ATU-203/-223 at NAAS Chase Field, Beeville, Texas; ATU-204/-213 at NAAS Chase Field, Beeville, Texas; ATU-206 at NAS Pensacola; ATU-212 at NAS Corpus Christi; ATU-222 at NAS Kingsville, Texas. Many of these squadrons flew the F9F-2/5 Panther and F9F-6 Cougar, although some did utilize the F9F-8 and -8B in the late 1950s.

The training command was restructured in May 1960. As part of the transition/reclassification, the following ATUs became training squadrons:

ATU-102 (redesignated ATU-202) became VT-21 Fighting Redhawks

ATU-212 became VT-22 Golden Eagles

ATU-222 became VT-23 Professionals (in 1958)

ATU-203 became VT-24 Bobcats

ATU-213 became VT-25 Cougars

ATU-223 became VT-26 Flying Tigers

The VT squadrons operated the F9F-8 and F9F-8T. VT-4 Mighty War Bucks also operated the single-seat F9F-8 and the two-seat F9F-8T for a period of time, and were the last training squadron to fly the Cougar. VT-31 Wise Owls, which trained jet crews for larger aircraft, also operated an F9F-8T.

## Marine Corps Training

The Marine Corps trained jet fighter pilots in VMFT-10/VMT-2/VMT-103 (F9F-5) and VMFT-20 (F9F-5).

## Support & Reserves

The Panther and Cougar were both featured in Navy test and evaluation squadrons as well as fleet support units. Panthers flew with at least 12 Fleet Air Service Squadrons (FASRONs); Naval Air Test Center (NATC), Patuxent River, Maryland; Naval Ordnance Test Station (NOTS), China Lake, California; Pacific Missile Range, Naval Air Test Facility (NATF) NAS Lakehurst, New Jersey; NAS Pt. Mugu, California; Guided Missile Groups One and Two (GMGRU-1 and -2); Fleet Air Gunnery Unit (FAGU), El Centro, California; Air Development Squadron Three (VX-3); VF(AW)-4, and VAH-1. Six Utility Squadrons, VU-1, -2, -4, -5, -7, and -10 and VCs-3 and -8 also flew F9Fs.

## Navy and Marine Corps Reserve Units

Navy and Marine Corps Reserve units were based at various air stations around the United States. Oftentimes the two services would share the same aircraft, so it was not uncommon to see a single tail designation. The following were Reserve units that operated the Panther or Cougar:

| | | |
|---|---|---|
| NATU Jacksonville, FL | 6F | F9F-6/8 |
| NAS Atlanta, GA | 7B | F9F-8 |
| NAS Columbus, OH | 7C | F9F-6 |

VMF-221, VMF-224

| | | |
|---|---|---|
| NAS Dallas, TX | 7D | F9F-6/6P/7 |

VF-701, -702

| | | |
|---|---|---|
| NAS Denver, CO | 7P | F9F-6/7 |

VF-711, -712, -713, -718

VMF-236

| | | |
|---|---|---|
| NAS Glenview, IL | 7V | F9F-4/6/6P/7/8B |
| NAS Los Alamitos, CA | 7L | F9F-6/6P |

VF-771, -772, -776, -777

VMF-123, -134, -241, -534

| | | |
|---|---|---|
| NAS Lincoln, NE | 7N | F9F-6 |

VMF-113

| | | |
|---|---|---|
| NAS Memphis, TN | 6M | F9F-6 |

VF-791, -792

VMF-124

| | | |
|---|---|---|
| NAS Miami, FL | 6H | F9F-6 |

VMF-142, -341

| | | |
|---|---|---|
| NAS Minneapolis, MN | 7E | F9F-5 |
| NAS New Orleans, LA | 7X | F9F-6/7/8 |
| NAS New York, NY | 7R | F9F-7/8 |
| NAS Olathe, KS | 7K | F9F-6/7/8 |
| NAS Spokane, WA | 5N | F9F-6 |
| NAS South Weymouth, MA | 7Z | F9F-6 |

VF-911, -912, -913, -914, -915, -917

VMF-217, -322

| | | |
|---|---|---|
| NAS Willow Grove, PA | 7W | F9F-6/7 |
| Blue Angels | | 2/5/6/8/8T |

# F9F PRODUCTION

## F9F PANTHER

| Model | Designation | BuNos | Number Produced |
|-------|-------------|-------|-----------------|
| G-75 | XF9F-1 | N/A | 0 |
| G-79 | XF9F-2 (K-1) | 122475, 122477 | 2 |
| G-79 | F9F-2 (K-4) | 122563, 122567, 125669<br>122570, 122572<br>123016–123019<br>123044–123067<br>123077–123086<br>123397–123713<br>125083–125155<br>127086–127215 | 564 |
| G-79 | XF9F-3 (K-2) | 122476 | 1 |
| G-79 | F9F-3 | 122560–122562<br>122564–122566<br>122568–122571<br>122573–122585<br>123020–123043<br>123068–123076 | 54 |
| G-79 | XF9F-4 (K-419) | 123084 | 1 |
| G-79 | F9F-4 | 125081<br>125156–125227<br>125913–125948 | 109 |
| G-79 | XF9F-5 (K-420) | 123085 | 1 |
| G-79 | F9F-5 | 125080–125082<br>125228–125313<br>125447–125476<br>125489–125499<br>125533–125648<br>125893–125912<br>125949–126256<br>126627–126672 | 616 |
| G-79 | F9F-5P (K-742) | 125314–125321<br>126265–126290<br>127471–127472 | 36 |
| | Total Panthers | | 1,385 |

## F9F COUGAR

| Model | Designation | BuNos | Number Produced |
|-------|-------------|-------|-----------------|
| G-93 | XF9F-6 | 126670–126672 | 3 |
| G-93 | F9F-6 (L-1) | 126257–126264<br>127216–127470<br>128055–128294<br>130920–131062 | 696 |
| G-93 | F9F-6P (L-1P) | 127473–127492<br>128295–128310<br>131252–131255<br>134446–134465 | 60 |
| G-93 | F9F-7 (L-1A) | 130752–130919 | 118 |
| G-99 (L-1C) | F9F-8 | 131063–131251<br>134234–134244<br>138823–138898<br>141030–141229<br>141648–141666<br>144271–144376 | 601 |
| G-105 | F9F-8P | 141668–141727<br>144377–144426 | 110 |
| G-105 | YF9F-8T (1XT) | 141667 | 1 |
| G-105 (Shop No. 1) | F9F-8T | 142437–142532<br>142954–143012<br>146342–146425<br>147270–147429 | 400 |
| | Total Cougars 1,988 | | |

Total F9F Aircraft Built          3,373

# F9F PANTHER KOREAN WAR DEPLOYMENTS

USS *Valley Forge* (CV-45), CVG-5
1 May 1950 to 1 December 1950
| | | |
|---|---|---|
| VF-51 | F9F-3 | S/100 |
| VF-52 | F9F-3 | S/200 |

USS *Philippine Sea* (CV-47), CVG-11
5 July 1950 to 26 March 1951
| | | |
|---|---|---|
| VF-111 | F9F-2 | V/100 |
| VF-112 | F9F-2 | V/200 |

USS *Leyte* (CV-32), CVG-3
6 September 1950 to 3 February 1951
| | | |
|---|---|---|
| VF-31 | F9F-2 | K/100 |

USS *Princeton* (CV-37), CVG-19
9 November 1950 to 29 May 1951
| | | |
|---|---|---|
| VF-191 | F9F-2 | B/200 |
| VC-61 Det. | F9F-2P | PP |

USS *Boxer* (CV-21), CVG-101
2 March 1951 to 24 October 1951
| | | |
|---|---|---|
| VF-721 | F9F-2B | A/100 |
| VF-821 | F9F-2B | A/200 |
| VC-61 Det. F | F9F-2P | PP |

USS *Bon Homme Richard* (CV-31), CVG-102
10 May 1951 to 17 December 1951
| | | |
|---|---|---|
| VF-781 | F9F-2B | D/100 |
| VC-61 Det. G | F9F-2P | PP |

USS *Princeton* (CV-37), CVG-19
31 May 1951 to 29 August 1951
| | | |
|---|---|---|
| VF-23 | F9F-2 | M/200 |
| VC-61 Det. | F9F-2P | PP |

USS *Essex* (CV-9), CVG-5
26 June 1951 to 25 March 1952
| | | |
|---|---|---|
| VF-51 | F9F-2 | S/100 |

USS *Antietam* (CV-36), CVG-15
8 September 1951 to 2 May 1952
| | | |
|---|---|---|
| VF-831 | F9F-2B | H/300 |
| VF-837 | F9F-2B | H/400 |
| VC-61 Det. D | F9F-2P | PP |

USS *Valley Forge* (CV-45), ATG-1
15 October 1951 to 3 July 1952
| | | |
|---|---|---|
| VF-111 | F9F-2B | V/100 |
| VF-52 | F9F-2B | S/200 |
| VC-61 Det. H | F9F-2P | PP |

USS *Philippine Sea* (CV-47), CVG-11
31 December 1951 to 8 August 1952
| | | |
|---|---|---|
| VF-112 | F9F-2 | V/200 |
| VC-61 Unit C | F9F-2P | PP |

USS *Boxer* (CV-21), CVG-2
28 February 1952 to 26 September 1952
| | | |
|---|---|---|
| VF-24 | F9F-2 | M/400 |
| VC-61 Det. A | F9F-2P | PP |

USS *Princeton* (CV-37), CVG-19
21 March 1952 to 3 November 1952
| | | |
|---|---|---|
| VF-191 | F9F-2 | B/100 |
| VC-61 Det. E | F9F-2P | PP |

USS *Bon Homme Richard* (CV-31), CVG-7
20 May 1952 to 8 January 1953
| | | |
|---|---|---|
| VF-71 | F9F-2 | L/100 |
| VF-72 | F9F-2 | L/200 |
| VC-61 Det. N | F9F-2P | PP |

USS *Essex* (CV-9), ATG-2
16 June 1952 to 13 January 1952
| | | |
|---|---|---|
| VF-23 | F9F-2 | M/100 |
| VF-821 | F9F-2 | A/200 |
| VC-61 Det. I | F9F-2P | PP |

USS *Kearsarge* (CV-33), CVG-101
11 August 1952 to 12 March 1953
| | | |
|---|---|---|
| VF-721 | F9F-2 | A/100 |

USS *Oriskany* (CV-34), CVG-102
15 September 1952 to 18 May 1953
| | | |
|---|---|---|
| VF-781 | F9F-5 | D/100 |
| VF-783 | F9F-5 | D/200 |

USS *Valley Forge* (CV-45), CVG-5
20 November 1952 to 25 June 1953
| | | |
|---|---|---|
| VF-51 | F9F-5 | S/100 |

| | | | | Deployments by Squadron | |
|---|---|---|---|---|---|
| VF-53 | F9F-5 | S/300 | | | |
| VC-61 Det. B | F9F-2P | PP | | VF-23 | 2 |
| | | | | VF-71 | 1 |
| USS *Philippine Sea* (CV-47), CVG-9 | | | | VF-151 | 1 |
| 15 December 1952 to 14 August 1953 | | | | VF-783 | 1 |
| VF-91 | F9F-2 | N/100 | | VF-24 | 1 |
| VF-93 | F9F-2 | N/300 | | VF-72 | 1 |
| VC-61 Det. M | F9F-2P | PP | | VF-153 | 1 |
| | | | | VF-821 | 1 |
| USS *Princeton* (CV-37), CVG-105 | | | | VF-31 | 1 |
| 24 January 1953 to 26 September 1953 | | | | VF-91 | 1 |
| VF-153 | F9F-5 | H/300 | | VF-154 | 1 |
| VF-154 | F9F-5 | H/400 | | VF-831 | 1 |
| VC-61 Det. D | F9F-2P | PP | | VF-51 | 3 |
| | | | | VF-92 | 1 |
| USS *Lake Champlain* (CV-39), CVG-4 | | | | VF-191 | 2 |
| 26 April 1953 to 4 December 1953 | | | | VF-837 | 1 |
| VF-111 | F9F-5 | V | | VF-52 | 3 |
| (Transferred to USS *Boxer* 30 June 1953) | | | | VF-111 | 4 |
| | | | | VF-721 | 2 |
| USS *Boxer* (CV-21), ATG-1 | | | | VC-61 | |
| 30 March 1953 to 28 November 1953 | | | | VF-53 | 1 |
| VF-52 | F9F-2 | S/200 | | VF-112 | 2 |
| VF-111 | F9F-5 | V/100 | | VF-781 | 2 |
| VF-151 | F9F-2 | H/300 | | *Det. | 13 |

# BIBLIOGRAPHY

### Books

Allen, Ned, *Dependable Engines: The Story of Pratt & Whitney* (Library of Flight, 2008).

Davis, Larry, *P-80 Shooting Star in Action* (Squadron/Signal Publications, 1980).

Doll, Thomas E., *USN/USMC Over Korea: U.S. Navy/Marine Corps Air Operations Over Korea, 1950-53* (Squadron/Signal Publications, 1988).

Francillon, Rene J., *Grumman Aircraft Since 1929* (Naval Institute Press, 1989).

Ginter, Steve, *Naval Fighters Number Two: McDonnell Banshee* (Ginter, 1980).

—. *Naval Fighters Number Four: F3D Skyknight* (Ginter, 1984).

—. *Naval Fighters Number Sixty: Grumman F9F Part 2: USMC Panthers* (Ginter Books, 2003).

—. *Naval Fighters Number Sixty-One: Grumman F9F Part 3: Navy Panthers Korea and Beyond* (Ginter Books, 2003).

—. *Naval Fighters Number Sixty-Nine: Navy & Marine Fleet Single-Seat F9F Cougar Squadrons* (Ginter Books, 2006).

Ginter, Steve, and Ron Picciani, *Naval Fighters Number Seven: North American FJ-1 Fury* (Ginter Books, 1983).

Hughes, Chris, and Walter Dranem, *North American F-86 SabreJet Day Fighters, WarbirdTech Series, Volume 3* (Specialty Press, 1996).

Kay, Anthony L., *Turbojet: History and Development 1930-1960, Volume 2* (The Crowood Press, 2007).

Kinzey, Bert, *F9F Panther in Detail & Scale* (Kalmbach Publishing, 1993).

—. *F9F Cougar in Detail & Scale* (Aero Publishers, Inc., 1983).

Lorell, Mark, *The U.S. Combat Aircraft Industry 1909-2000: Structure, Competition, Innovation* (RAND, National Defense Research Institute, 2003).

Lorell, Mark A., and Hugh. P. Levaux, *The Cutting Edge: A Half Century of U.S. Fighter Aircraft R&D* (RAND, Project Air Force, 1998).

Marriott, Leo, *Jets at Sea: Naval Aviation in Transition, 1945-1955* (Pen & Sword Aviation, 2008).

Meyer, Corwin, *Naval Fighters Number Fifty-Nine: Grumman F9F Panther, Part One: Development, Testing, Structures* (Ginter Books, 2002).

—. *Naval Fighters Number Sixty-Six: Grumman F9F Cougar, Part 1: Design, Testing, Structures and Blue Angels* (Ginter Books, 2005).

*Corky Meyer's Flight Journal: A Test Pilot's Tales of Dodging Disasters—Just in Time* (Specialty Press, 2006).

McDowell, Ernest, *FR-1 Fireball Mini in Action* (Squadron/Signal, 1995).

Pace, Steve, *Air Force Legends Number 208: Bell Aircraft P-59 Airacomet* (Ginter Books, 2000).

Pavelec, Sterling Michael, *The Jet Race and the Second World War* (Praeger Security International, 2007).

Schnitzer, George, Panthers *Over Korea* (Publish America, 2007).

Sullivan, Jim, *F9F Panther/Cougar in Action* (Squadron/Signal Publications, 1982).

Thomason, Tommy H., *U.S. Naval Air Superiority: Development of Shipborne Jet Fighters 1 9 4 3 - 1 9 6 2* (Specialty Press, 2007).

Treadwell, Terry C., *Ironworks: The Story of Grumman and Its Aircraft* (Tempus Publishing, 2000).

**Government Reports and Documents**

Naval Air Test Center Report, Project TED No. BIS 21171, *Special Report of Model YF9F-8, BUNO 131067, Shipboard Carrier Suitability Trials With External Stores* (Flight Test Division, 5 October 1955).

NAVAER SD-415 "Detail Specification for Model XF9F-1 Airplane Class VFN(M)(Monoplane)(Jet Propulsion), 17 January 1946.

*Report of the Joint Fighter Conference: NAS Patuxent River, MD, 16-23 October 1944* (Schiffer Military History, 1998).

RAE Report N.A.D. 14, dated January 1949, "Effects of Layout and Design of Future Carrier Operating Undercarriageless Aircraft."

Royal Aircraft Establishment (RAE) Report No. N.A. 198, dated February 1950, "Landing Experiments With Undercarriageless Aircraft on a Flexible Deck."

*Publications, Journals, Magazines, and Articles*

*BIS Trials,* Naval Aviation News, pp. 27-28 (March 1953).

# ENDNOTES

[i] Pavelec, Sterling Michael, *The Jet Race and the Second World War*, pp. 2-7 (Praeger Security International, 2007).

[ii] Neufeld, Jacob, George M. Watson, Jr., and David Chenweth, Editors, *Technology and the Air Force: A Retrospective Assessment*, essay, James O. Young, "Riding England's Coattails: The Army Air Forces and the Turbojet Revolution", pp. 3-7 (Air Force History and Museums Program 1997)(referenced as *Technology and the Air Force*). A good discussion of Frank Whittle and development of the British turbojet can be found in John Golley's *Genesis of the Jet: Frank Whittle and the Invention of the Jet Engine* (Airlife, 2004).

[iii] A good discussion of this event can be found in Constant, Edward W., *The Origins of the Turbojet Revolution*, p. 193 (Johns Hopkins University Press, 1980).

[iv] *The Jet Race and the Second World War*, p. 39.

[v] *The Jet Race and the Second World War*, pp. 162-168.

[vi] *The Jet Race and the Second World War*, p. 17; Constant, Edward W., *The Origins of the Turbojet Revolution*, pp. 151-177, 244, 271 (Johns Hopkins University Press, 1980).

[vii] *The Jet Race and the Second World War*, pp. 84-85.

[viii] For a discussion of the L-1000, see *Technology and the Air Force*, pp. 16-17.

[ix] Australian Academy of Science, Biographical Memiors—Edward George Bowen, www.science.org.au/academy/memoirs/bowen.htm

[x] *The Jet Race and the Second World War*, pp. 89-90, 129-132; Pace, Steve, *Air Force Legends Number 208: Bell Aircraft P-59 Airacomet* (Ginter Books, 2000).

[xi] *Technology and the Air Force*, pp. 26-27; *The Jet Race and the Second World War*, pp. 138-143. See also Davis, Larry, *P-80 Shooting Star in Action* (Squadron/Signal Publications, 1980).

[xii] For an excellent discussion of U.S. Air Force jet bomber development, see Alwyn T. Lloyd's, *Boeing B-47 Stratojet*, pp. 4-19 (Specialty Press, 2005).

[xiii] *The Jet Race and the Second World War*, p. 144.

[xiv] McDowell, Earnest, *FR-1 Fireball* (Squadron/Signal Publications, 1995).

[xv] Thomason, Tommy H., *U.S. Naval Air Superiority: The Development of Shipborne Jet Fighters, 1943–1962*, pp. 28-30 (Specialty Press, 2007). Thomason provides an excellent overview of the early development of U.S. Navy jet fighters.

[xvi] *United States Naval Aviation 1910-1995*, Appendix 5 (Naval Historical Center).

[xvii] Francillon, Rene, J., *Grumman Aircraft Since 1929*, pp. 315, 316 (Naval Institute Press 1989). See also BuAer Scientific Historical (Aer-1203), "Initial Steps in Development of the XF9F-2, XF3D-1, and XF10F-1 Aircraft," p. 1 (12 December 1955).

[xviii] BuAer Scientific Historical (Aer-1203), "Initial Steps in Development of XF9F-2, XF3D-1, and XF10F-1 Aircraft", p. 1 (12 December 1955). However, because the F4U did not typically deploy off of carriers, and in fact did not until December 1944, it was the F6F Hellcat that flew the majority of the Navy carrier night fighter missions.

[xix] The companies who received the Navy's 20 June 1945 letter were: Chance Vought, Grumman, Douglas, North American, Northrop, Lockheed, Consolidated-Vultee, Bell, and Goodyear. Boeing, Curtiss-Wright, and Republic were invited in July to submit proposals. Five companies declined to submit any proposal, due to either heavy work commitments or a lack of interest in night fighters. BuAer letter Aer-E-11-EHV, VF(N), dated 20 June 1945.

[xx] BuAer letter Aer-E-11-EHV, VF(N), dated 20 June 1945.

[xxi] Francillon, Rene J., *Grumman Aircraft Since 1929*, p. 550.

[xxii] BuAer letter Aer-E-11-EHV, VF(N), dated 20 June 1945.

[xxiii] BuAer Scientific Historical (Aer-1203), "Initial Steps in Development of the XF9F-2, XF3D-1, and XF10F-1 Aircraft," p. 1 (12 December 1955).

[xxiv] Thomason, Tommy H., *U.S. Naval Air Superiority: The Development of Shipborne Jet Fighters, 1943–1962*, p. 35 (Specialty Press, 2007).

[xxv] Corky Meyer discusses his thoughts on why Grumman was late to enter the jet race in his book, *Corky Meyer's Flight Journal: A Test Pilot's Tales of Dodging Disasters—Just in Time*, pp. 176, 177 (Specialty Press, 2006).

[xxvi] For a discussion of the various Grumman turbojet projects, *see* Francillon, Rene J., *Grumman Aircraft Since 1929*, pp. 171, 314-315.

[xxvii] Thomason, Tommy H., *U.S. Naval Air Superiority: The Development of Shipborne Jet Fighters, 1943–1962*, pp. 56-57 (Specialty Press, 2007); Report, Initial Steps in Development of XF9F-2, XF3D-1, and XF10F-1 Aircraft, BuAer Scientific Historical (Aer-1203), dated 12 December 1955.

[xxviii] Grumman Design 79 Study. See also, Kinzey, Bert, *F9F Panther*, *Volume 15, Detail & Scale*, pp. 5-7 (Kalmbach Books, 1993).

[xxix] Model XF9F-2 Proposed Program for Preliminary Aerodynamic Evaluation, dated 17 September 1946.

[xxx] Meyer, Corwin "Corky", *Grumman F9F Panther, Part One: Development, Testing, Structures, Naval Fighter Series Number 59*, p. 1 (Ginter Books, 2002).

[xxxi] Meyer, *Grumman F9F Panther*, p. 1.

[xxxii] The Navy required that the Americanized Nene design operate on gasoline as well as kerosene fuels. This requirement was especially difficult because it required redesign and rebuilding of the fuel pumps, and that this redesign was to be undertaken using all American parts and sources. *The Pratt & Whitney Aircraft Story*, p. 168-169, Pratt & Whitney (August 1950).

[xxxiii] Pilot's Manual for Navy Models F9F-2, -3 Airplanes, AN 01-85FGA-1 p. 1 (15 January 1951).

[xxxiv] The Panther's hydraulic wing fold mechanism was not strong enough to fold the wings with fuel in the tip tanks, so in all cases when the Panther was aboard the carrier, the wings had to be folded prior to refueling. Since the Panther did not have a single-point refueling system found in later aircraft, the deck crewmen had to use a specially configured ladder to refuel each wingtip tank individually.

[xxxv] Francillon, Rene J., *Grumman Aircraft Since 1929*, p. 317 (Naval Institute Press, 1989). A good discussion of this flight is also contained in Corky Meyer's books, *Corky Meyer's Flight Journal: A Test Pilot's Tales of Dodging Disasters—Just in Time*, at pages 176-179, and *Naval Fighters Number Fifty-Nine: Grumman F9F Panther, Part One: Development, Testing, Structures*, at pages 3-6.

[xxxvi] Meyer, *Grumman F9F Panther*, pp. 5-6.

[xxxvii] Meyer, *Grumman F9F Panther*, pp. 5-7.

xxxviii Silsbee, Nathaniel F., "Grumman "Panther"—Carrier Fighter with Claws", Aero Digest pp. 28, 30 (July 1948).

xxxix Silsbee, p. 30.

xl Meyer, Corwin, *Naval Fighters Number Fifty-Nine: Grumman F9F Panther, Part One: Development, Testing, Structures*, p. 10 (Ginter Books, 2002)

xli Meyer, *Grumman F9F* Panther, pp. 12 -15.

xlii Francillon, Rene J., *Grumman Aircraft Since 1929*, p. 329 (Naval Institute Press, 1989).

xliii Comments, Walter Spangenberg, October 2009.

xliv Action Report, USS *Philippine Sea* (CV-47), 1 January to 1 February 1951, p. 14.

xlv Action Report, USS *Philippine Sea* (CV-47), 1 January to 1 February 1951, p. 14.

xlvi Comments, Walter Spangenberg, October 2009.

xlvii Comments, Walter Spangenberg, October 2009.

xlviii Action Report, USS *Antietam* (CV-36), for the period from 15 October through 16 November 1951, p. 15. For this deployment, the *Antietam* was teamed with Carrier Air Group 15.

xlix Action Report, USS *Antietam* (CV-36), for the period from 15 October through 16 November 1951, p. 15.

l Comments, Walter Spangenberg, October 2009.

li Action Report, USS *Philippine Sea* (CV-47), 1 January to 1 February 1951, p. 11.

lii Action Report, USS *Philippine Sea* (CV-47), 1 January to 1 February 1951, p. 11.

liii Action Report, USS *Philippine Sea* (CV-47), 1 January to 1 February 1951, p. 11.

liv Action Report, USS *Philippine Sea* (CV-47), 1 January to 1 February 1951, pp. 11-12.

lv Pilot's Manual for Navy Models F9F-2, -3 Airplanes, AN 01-85FGA-1, p. 57, 64, 65 (15 January 1951).

lvi Pilot's Manual for Navy Models F9F-2, -3 Airplanes, AN 01-85FGA-1, p. 57, 64, 65 (15 January 1951).

lvii Comments, Walter Spangenberg, October 2009.

lviii Schnitzer, George, *Panthers Over Korea*, p. 108 (Publish America, 2007).

lix Corky Meyer discusses this in detail in his book *Grumman F9F Panther*, at pages 17-19.

lx Schnitzer, *Panthers Over Korea*, p. 130.

lxi Schnitzer, *Panthers Over Korea*, p. 130.

lxii "Navy Rockets Hit Reds", Naval Aviation News, pp. 8-9 (October 1950).

lxiii Action Report of Carrier Air Group One Hundred Two for Period 8 August 1951 to 5 September 1951, p. 6. During this deployment, CVG-102 was embarked aboard USS *Bon Homme Richard* (CV-31).

lxiv Ginter, Steve, *Grumman F9F Part Two: USMC Panthers*, *Naval Fighters Number Sixty*, p. 11 (Ginter Books, 2003).

lxv Action Report, USS *Princeton* (CV-37) and Carrier Air Group 15, for period 13 April through 19 May 1953, pp. 6-7.

lxvi Action Report, USS *Princeton* (CV-37) and Carrier Air Group 15, for period 13 April through 19 May 1953, p. 7.

lxvii Francillon, *Grumman Aircraft*, p. 323.

lxviii Treadwell, Terry C., *Ironworks: The Story of Grumman and its Aircraft*, p. 98 (Tempus Publishing, 2000).

lxix Meyer, *Grumman F9F* Panther, pp. 27-28.

lxx Meyer, *Grumman F9F* Panther, pp. 27-28.

lxxi Project TED No. PTR AD-349, F9F-4 Airplane With Supercirculation Boundary Layer Control; Performance, Flying Qualities, Landbased And Shipboard Carrier Suitability Evaluation, letter report No. 1, final report, dated 2 June 1954.

lxxii United States Naval Aviation 1910-1995, Appendix 25, "Carrier, Carrier Based Squadron, Non-Carrier Based Squadron Deployments During the Korean War" (Naval Historical Center).

lxxiii Dorr, Robert F., *"Panther on the Prowl: The U.S. Navy's First Jet 'Kills'"*, Combat Aircraft, Vol. 7, No. 8. pp. 62-66 (September 2006).

lxxiv Dorr, *"Panther on the Prowl: The U.S. Navy's First Jet 'Kills'"*, p. 66.

lxxv Dorr, p. 66.

lxxvi Action Report of Carrier Air Group Five, 18 August 1951–19 September 1951, p. 17.

lxxvii "Swept-Wing MiG-15 in Korea", Naval Aviation News, pp. 14-15.

lxxviii Gordon, Yefin, *MiG-15 Fagot: Volume 40* (WarbirdTech Series) (Specialty Press, 2005); Krylov, Leonid, and Yuriy, Tepsurkaev, *Soviet MiG-15 Aces of the Korean War* (Osprey Publishing, 2008).

lxxix Action Report, USS *Philippine Sea* (CV-47), pp. 13-14, for the period 1 November to 31 December 1950.

lxxx Action Report, USS *Philippine Sea* (CV-47), pp. 13-14, for the period 1 November to 31 December 1950.

lxxxi For an excellent discussion of this event, see Kum-Sok, No, *A MiG-15 to Freedom: Memoir of the Wartime North Korean Defector Who First Delivered the Secret Fighter Jet to the Americans in 1953* (McFarland, 2007).

lxxxii Ginter, Steve, *Grumman F9F Part 3: Navy* Panthers: *Korea and Beyond*, p. 78 (Ginter Books, 2003).

lxxxiii Schnitzer, *Panthers Over Korea*, p. 64.

lxxxiv Action Report of Carrier Air Group One Hundred Two for the Period of 28 October through 22 November 1952, p. VI-1 through VI-3.

lxxxv Interview, CAPT. Royce Williams (USN, Ret.), 22 November 2009.

lxxxvi Action Report of Carrier Air Group One Hundred Two for the Period of 28 October through 22 November 1952, p. VI-3 through VI-4.

lxxxvii Action Report of Carrier Air Group One Hundred Two for the Period of 28 October through 22 November 1952, p. VI-4.

lxxxviii Davis, Lyle E., "The 15 Minute War at 26,000 Feet", The Paper, July 14, 2005.

lxxxix Korean Air War and Surrounding Events, compiled by Stephen L. Sewell, at www.korean-war.com/AirChronology.html; Department of Defense Korean War Air Loss Database.

xc Action Report, USS *Philippine Sea* (CV-47), for the period 1 January to 1 February 1951, F-9F-2 Operating Procedures During Korean Campaign, pp. 6-7.

xci Action Report, USS *Philippine Sea* (CV-47), for the period 1 January to 1 February 1951, F-9F-2 Operating Procedures During Korean Campaign, pp. 6-7.

xcii Schnitzer, George, *Panthers Over Korea* (Publish America, 2007).

xciii Action Report, USS *Philippine Sea* (CV-47), for the period 1 November through 31 December 1950, CVG-11 Operational Summary for the Period 1 November through December 31, 1950, pp. 1-2.

[xciv] Action Report, USS *Philippine Sea* (CV-47), for the period 1 November through 31 December 1950, CVG-11 Operational Summary for the Period 1 November through December 31, 1950, p. 2.

[xcv] Action Report, USS *Philippine Sea* (CV-47), for the period 1 November through 31 December 1950, CVG-11 Operational Summary for the Period 1 November through December 31, 1950, pp. 13-15.

[xcvi] Narrative Action Report, USS *Leyte* (CV-32), for the period 1 December through 31 December 1950, pp. 1, 2, 11, 12.

[xcvii] Narrative Action Report, USS *Leyte* (CV-32), for the period 1 December through 31 December 1950, pp. 11-12.

[xcviii] Cagle, Malcom W., and Frank A. Manson, *The Sea War in Korea*, p. 461 (Naval Institute Press, 1957).

[xcix] Carrier Air Group Nineteen, Action Report for Period 26 February 1951 through 2 April 1951, pp. 1, 2.

[c] Carrier Air Group Nineteen, Action Report for Period 26 February 1951 through 2 April 1951, pp. 2, 3.

[ci] Carrier Air Group Nineteen, Action Report for Period 26 February 1951 through 2 April 1951, p. 4.

[cii] Action Report, Air Task Group Two, for the period 25 November 1952 through 13 January 1953, pp. 3, 6-7.

[ciii] Action Report, Air Task Group Two, for the period 25 November 1952 through 13 January 1953, pp. 10-11.

[civ] Action Report, USS *Princeton* (CV-37), 4 July through 6 August 1952, pp. 11-12. The Report stated that Air Group strikes had a normal composition of 8 to 12 jet aircraft for initial flak suppression, 12 to 28 Corsairs for secondary flak suppression and/or bombing, and 8 to 14 ADs for the major bombing effort. Coordination of the strike elements was achieved by launching the conventional prop aircraft about one-half hour before the jet launch and affecting a rendezvous of the two types about 10 to 15 miles from the target area.

[cv] Summary Action Report, Carrier Air Group Twelve (formerly ATG 102), for the period 28 October 1952 through 22 April 1953, p. 15.

[cvi] Summary Action Report, Carrier Air Group Twelve (formerly ATG 102), for the period 28 October 1952 through 22 April 1953, p. 16.

[cvii] Action Report, USS *Princeton* (CV-37) and Carrier Air Group Fifteen, for the period 9 June through 3 August 1953, p. 17.

[cviii] Action Report, Carrier Air Group Nineteen, for the Period 18 January 1951 through 15 February 1951, p. 2. Three F9F-2P aircraft were deployed as part of a VC-61 detachment. The photo Panthers flew 25 photographic missions providing pre- and post-strike coverage of 176 bridges located along 600 miles of enemy transportation routes. Bridge targets were briefed from photographs and the pilots were given target pictures for use during the strike missions.

[cix] Action Report, USS *Essex* (CV-9), for the period 13 December 1951 through 3 February 1952, pp. 14-15.

[cx] Action Report, USS *Essex* (CV-9), for the period 13 December 1951 through 3 February 1952, pp. 14-15.

[cxi] The Official Ted Williams Web Site, www.tedwillaims.com.

[cxii] Action Report, Carrier Air Group Five, for the period 18 August through 19 September 1951, p. 5.

[cxiii] Bedford, Alan, "Panthers Over Korea" FlyPast Jan. 1999: 74, 77. *See also* Bedford, Alan, "Panthers Over Korea" Dec. FlyPast 1998:98.

[cxiv] BuAer Letter, Aer-E-11-JFS, PTR 1120—Evaluation of German Aircraft, dated 24 July 1945. NA83(1)/VMe-262 PTR 1120 (FT), Evaluation of German Aircraft—Final Report on Forwarding of (dated 13 June 1946). Project pilots included Lt. Col. M. E. Carl, UMSC, Lt. (j.g.) McClelland, UNS, and Senior Project Officer Cdr. E. M. Owen, USN. Flight tests evaluated the Me-262 and Ar 234 aircraft beginning in October 1945 and concluding in late January 1946.

[cxv] For an excellent discussion of the American efforts to obtain German jet technology after World War II, see *The Jet Race and the Second World War*, pp. 149-156.

[cxvi] Francillon, *Grumman Aircraft*, p. 551.

[cxvii] Francillon, *Grumman Aircraft*, pp. 345, 377. The Jaguar was the outgrowth of Grumman's early efforts to develop a swept-wing version of the XF9F-2/XF9F-3. Design 83 retained little in common with the XF9F-2/XF9F-3 other than the forward fuselage, cockpit, and J42 turbojet engine.

[cxviii] Thomason, Tommy H., *U.S. Naval Air Superiority: The Development of Shipborne Jet Fighters, 1943–1962*, p. 128 (Specialty Press, 2007). The author provides an excellent discussion of the development of swept-wing jet fighters during the 1947-1951 timeframe.

[cxix] *U.S. Naval Air Superiority: The Development of Shipborne Jet Fighters, 1943–1962*, p. 128.

[cxx] Francillon, *Grumman Aircraft*, pp. 334-335.

[cxxi] Grumman document, "The Flex Deck", undated.

[cxxii] Flight Manual for the F9F-6 Cougar, pp. 81-82.

[cxxiii] Flight Manual for the F9F-6 Cougar, p. 82-84.

[cxxiv] Naval Air Test Center Report, Project TED No. BIS 21171, Model YF9F08, BuNo 131067, Special Report of Shipboard Carrier Suitability Trials with External Stores (Flight Test Division), dated 5 October 1955. pp. 2-3.

[cxxv] Naval Air Test Center Report, Project TED No. BIS 21171, Model YF9F08, BuNo 131067, Special Report of Shipboard Carrier Suitability Trials with External Stores (Flight Test Division), dated 5 October 1955. pp. 2-3.

[cxxvi] Ginter, Steve, *Naval Fighters Number Sixty-Nine: Navy and Marine Fleet Single-Seat F9F* Cougar *Squadrons* (Ginter Books, 2006).

[cxxvii] Francillon, *Grumman Aircraft*, pp. 341-342.

[cxxviii] Francillon, *Grumman Aircraft*, pp. 339-342.

[cxxix] Thomason, *U.S. Naval Air Superiority*, p. 139-141.

[New] Meyer, Corwin, *Naval Fighters Number Sixty-Six, Grumman F9F-6/7/8 Cougar, Part One*, p. 24 (Ginter Books 2005)

[cxxx] Meyer, Corwin "Corky", *Naval Fighters Number Sixty-Six Part One: Grumman F9F-6/7/8* Cougar, p. 23 and p. 24 (Ginter Books, 2005).

# INDEX

Halford H-1B turbojet, 16, 27, 30
Hawkins, Lt. Larry, 108
Heagerty, Lt. Hal, 142
Heinkel, Ernst, 9, 10, 42
Heinkel-Strahltriebwerk,
High Velocity Aerial Rockets (HVAR), 63, 67-71, 74,
    99-101, 103
Hispano-Suiza, 64
HMS *Triumph* (R. 16), 90, 104
HMS *Warrior* (R. 31), 143
Holm, LCdr. Stan, 96
Hoskins, Lt. G. W., 142

## J

Jolly Rogers, 127
Junkers Motoren (Jumo), 9
    Jumo 004B, 9, 10, 45, 79, 103

## K

Karanik, John, 30, 31
Keystone Aircraft Company, 20
Kimpo AB, 93
Komet, 42
Kotcher, Ezra, 10

## L

Low Altitude Bombing System (LABS), 73, 134
Lamb, LCdr. William E., 94
Lambert, 1st Sgt. Larry, 42
Lanham, Cdr. Harvey, 90
Lockheed Aircraft Corporation
    L-1000 turbojet engine (XJ37), 10
    L-133 Starjet, 10, 12
        XP-38 Lightning, 10
        XP-49, 10
        XP-80 Lulu Belle, 12
        P-80 Shooting Star, 12, 13, 19, 21, 31, 32, 92, 93
        T-33 Trainer, 21, 49, 60, 72, 136
        TO-2/TV-2, 21
        T2V-1 Seastar, 136
Loening, Grover, 20
Loening Aircraft Engineering Corporation, 20
Longworth, Lt. R. L., 142

## M

Magda, LCdr. John, 142
Mahood, Lt. Ed, 142
Marine Corps Air Station (MCAS) Cherry Point, 14
Marine Corps Air Station (MCAS) El Toro, 135
Marine Corps Air Station (MCAS) Miami, 78
Marine Corps Air Station (MCAS) Miramar, 61
Martin, Sir James, 42
Martin-Baker Company, 42
Massachusetts Institute of Technology, 30
McDonnell Aircraft Company, 13
    XP-67 Bat, 14
    XFD-1 Phantom, 13, 14, 16, 19, 142, 146

FH-1 Phantom, 13, 14, 18, 19, 21, 27
F2H-1 Banshee, 6, 9, 14, 17, 18, 19, 21, 22, 31, 74,
    91, 110, 113, 131
McNamara, Robert S., 16
Metropolitan Vickers (Metrovick), 9, 45, 79, 103
Metsger, Cdr. A. B., 27, 112
Meyer, Corwin "Corky," 30, 33, 34, 36, 39, 40, 66, 81-
    83, 112, 128, 138, 141
Middleton, Lt. (j.g.) John D., 94-97
MiG-15 Fagot, 8, 91-94, 97-99, 113, 114, 128, 138
Moore, Lt. John, 120
Muroc Dry Lake Army Air Force Test Center, 12, 18

## N

NAN Comandante Espora, 138
NACA (National Advisory Committee for
    Aeronautics), 11
NATC (Naval Air Test Center), 18, 19, 22, 23, 38, 39,
    41, 58, 68, 73, 81, 82, 114, 117, 120, 126, 128-130
NATO (North Atlantic Treaty Organization)
Naval Air Station (NAS) Cecil Field, 21, 22, 129
Naval Air Station (NAS) China Lake, 57, 68-71, 73, 76, 137
Naval Air Station (NAS) El Centro, 137
Naval Air Station (NAS) Kingsville, 137
Naval Air Station (NAS) Minneapolis, 58, 85
Naval Air Station (NAS) Miramar, 61
Naval Air Station (NAS) Pensacola, 20, 56, 60, 108, 145
Naval Air Station (NAS) Point Mugu, 57
Naval Air Test Center (NATC) Patuxent River, 6, 18,
    19, 22, 36, 108, 120
North American, 7, 12, 14, 16, 17, 19, 78, 83, 112, 121,
    127, 138
    B-45 Tornado, 12
    XP-86 Sabre, 8, 17, 19, 93, 112, 138
    F-86 Sabre, 8, 17, 19, 93, 108, 110, 112, 113, 138
    FJ-1 Fury, 14, 16-18, 19, 21, 27, 31, 38, 60, 78, 113, 121
    FJ-2 Fury, 78, 114, 138
    AJ-2 Savage, 116, 121
    A3J Vigilante, 73, 135
Northrop Corporation, 10, 21
Northrop Grumman, 21

## O

Ohain, Hans von, 8, 9
Oliphant, Lt. Ed, 142
Owens, Ted, 18

## P

Pakhomkin, Sr. Lt., 97
Parker, Lt. Robert E., 94
"Peepin' Tom", 59
Pierced Steel Planking (PSP), 107
Plog, Lt. (j.g.) Leonard "Len," 90, 91
Poor, Edmund W., 9, 12, 20, 45, 79, 94, 98, 103, 112
Pratt & Whitney, 16, 27, 29-32, 39, 49, 60, 78, 79, 81, 83,
    112, 118

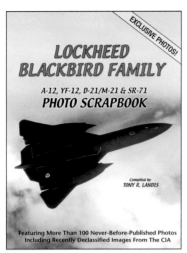
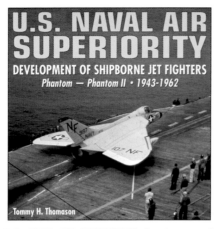
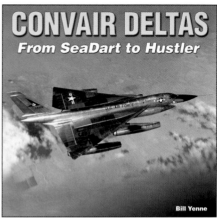
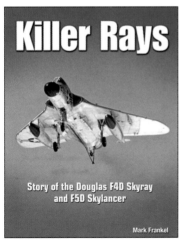
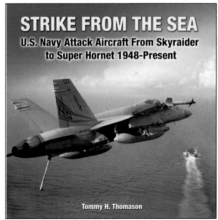